# OPPORTU

| | | DATE DUE | | |
|---|---|---|---|---|
| | | | | |
| | | | | |
| | | | | |
| | | | | |
| | | | | |
| | | | | |
| | | | | |
| | | | | |
| | | | | |
| | | | | |
| | | | | |

DISCARD

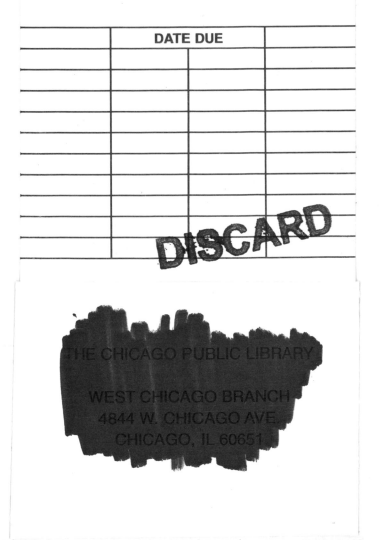

# OPPORTUNITIES in

# Fire Protection Services Careers

## REVISED EDITION

RONNY J. COLEMAN

## *VGM Career Books*

*Chicago   New York   San Francisco   Lisbon   London   Madrid   Mexico City
Milan   New Delhi   San Juan   Seoul   Singapore   Sydney   Toronto*

**Library of Congress Cataloging-in-Publication Data**

Coleman, Ronny J.
    Opportunities in fire protection services careers / Ronny J. Coleman—Rev. ed.
        p.  cm.—(VGM opportunities series)
    Includes bibliographical references.
    ISBN 0-07-140583-6
        1. Fire prevention—Vocational guidance.    2. Fire prevention—United States—
Vocational guidance.    I. Title.    II. Series.

    TH9119 .C65  2003
    628.9'2'02373—dc21                                                      2002034349

1  2  3  4  5  6  7  8  9  0     LBM/LBM     2  1  0  9  8  7  6  5  4  3

ISBN 0-07-140583-6

Interior design by Rattray Design

This book is printed on acid-free paper.

# Contents

# Foreword

I BEGAN MY career as a volunteer firefighter in a small community in Nebraska. Upon entering the fire service, I had no idea of the impact that decision would have on my life. It only took the first response to a significant incident to understand that fire fighting meant everything about service over self. In what other profession can you respond to the most traumatic and chaotic situation, and through effective teamwork and giving of yourself physically and mentally, make such a difference? In many situations, the action you take will have an impact on the people you have helped for the rest of their lives. I think there are few professions, if any, that provide such a degree of fulfillment.

As I have moved from being a volunteer firefighter to a career firefighter, have been successful enough to be promoted up through the ranks to become chief of a department, and have served as president of the International Association of Fire Chiefs, I have realized that there is much more to the field of the fire service than simply putting out fires. The world of the fire service has changed over the course of my career. During the last thirty years, we have seen the industry go from largely a suppression-based agency to one that provides a variety of services—from state-of-the-art emergency field medicine to hazardous materials mitigation to our expanded mission of disaster preparedness and response to terrorist events.

These changes will pale in comparison to what will happen during your career in the fire service. Our ability to utilize technology, to utilize more sophisticated analysis, and to elevate the level of professionalism will be dictated by the people who are entering the fire service today.

It is an exciting time to be part of the fire service. Although there will be many changes in the future in types of services and how we deliver them, our traditions and heritage will remain. That is what makes this profession so great.

Randy R. Bruegman
Fire Chief
President, IAFC, 2002–2003

# Acknowledgments

THE FIRE PROFESSION is truly an international endeavor. Almost anywhere you go you will find a local fire station. It is a profession that has evolved over time and will continue to evolve as future challenges are presented to the fire service. This is now my fortieth year in the fire service. I was at one time an entry-level firefighter; today as a chief officer, I can look backward with a strong sense of respect for the past and, as a planner, I can look forward to what is likely to happen in the near future.

In previous editions of this book, I have named names of individuals who have provided me with motivation and information. However, I would like this edition to be dedicated in a different fashion.

On September 11, 2001, a very large number of firefighters lost their lives in an event that some say is the most significant tragedy to impact the fire service. I agree and disagree within the same breath. My disagreement is based on the fact that there have been tragedies in the past relative to this profession, but people have forgotten them. The events that shook New York, the Pentagon, and Shanksville, Pennsylvania, demand a lot of attention now, but may well be forgotten in the future.

Therefore, I would like to dedicate this book to all firefighters everywhere and for all time. It is my desire that we recognize the contributions and legacies of each and every one of them. It is impossible to name them all, but my experience has shown that some of you may already know whom I am referring to. Many individuals seek a fire service career because a member of their family is already there. It is my strongest desire that those in the next generation of the fire service have a sense of respect for that past as they proceed forth with their own careers.

# 1

# The History of
# Fire Protection

It has been said that fire was the foundation of civilization. When human beings first were exposed to fire they feared it, but they soon learned that it could be an ally as well as an enemy. Archaeologists tell us that the first uses of fire were to provide warmth and to prepare food. Fire quickly became useful in the smelting of metals and the potting of clay. Later, fire was used as a defense and sometimes as an early weapon of war.

Originally fire was considered a gift of the gods and was held as an object of religious significance. In early societies, the maker and keeper of the fire was a very important person. In Greek mythology, for example, the gods condemned Prometheus for giving mortals the use of fire. Flame was considered symbolic of the process of change, death, and rebirth. The myth of the phoenix is based on the idea that flame not only destroys but builds as well.

Flame was and still is used in sacred rites. Have you ever noticed, for example, how we use candles to celebrate birthdays and special events? Fire is the giver of life in the form of warmth and industry. But it is also a fearsome demon that can destroy life and property unless it is properly handled and understood.

The fire service has a good image, but many people have misconceptions of what fire protection is really all about. For example, there is a lot of publicity given to the fire fighting side of fire protection. That's the exciting, glamorous, and adventurous side of the occupation, but it is not an accurate picture of the entire field. Fire protection has evolved from some very simple concepts into a multibillion-dollar-a-year enterprise, of which fire fighting is only a small segment.

You are probably reading this book because you are thinking about entering the fire service profession. People in fire service jobs have the responsibility to keep fire under control. Before we explore the details of the jobs involved in fire protection, we will examine its historical development.

You may be surprised to find that many of the events and people you have read about in your history classes have had something to do with the development of the field of fire protection. At this point, let's see how far we have come in fire protection. It might tell us a lot about how far we are going to go in the future—the future that will contain your career.

## Ancient Flames

The earliest recorded history of an individual who took fire protection seriously speaks of a man named Hero, a Greek scientist living in Alexandria, Egypt. Around 1500 B.C. he invented the first fire pump, which was a giant syringe used to squirt water at a fire. Fire had already proven its ability to be an adversary. As people moved into walled cities for protection, they became vulnerable to the spread of uncontrolled fire. Some of the early cities were literally burned to the ground. Many of the greatest treasures of early civilization, such as the Great Library in Alexandria, were destroyed by fire.

The first recorded indication that society was concerned about combating fire on a large scale was during the reign of Caesar Augustus in Rome. There, in 24 B.C., the emperor formed a group of firefighters from the slaves. This group was called the *Vigiles*. They fought a great fire in Rome in 7 B.C. Their motto, Semper Vigilans (Always Vigilant), is the foundation of the idea that fire protection requires a conscious dedication to controlling the phenomenon of fire. Unfortunately Nero, a later emperor of Rome, didn't believe in fire prevention, for legend says that he allowed the city to burn while he played the fiddle.

As cities grew larger, so did the need for fire protection. One of the greatest fears of the early city dwellers was the cry of "Fire!"

In A.D. 872 the French passed a *curfew*, the first fire prevention law. Today, when we use the word curfew, it means that you have to be off the streets at a certain time. But the term originally comes from the French word meaning to "cover fire." The curfew law was based on the need to make sure that all cooking and heating fires were either out or under control before people went to sleep.

William the Conqueror passed another major curfew law in 1066. In 1177 the Parliament of England required that all the shacks that had built up around the Canterbury Cathedral be torn down and removed because they were a fire hazard to the church. In 1189 a law was passed that required all new buildings to have stone walls and slate roofs.

## Fire Prevention Awareness

The emphasis in those days was on fire prevention. The organized fire fighting concept that started in Rome never really caught on, perhaps because slavery went out of style and freemen were more interested in business and industry than in fighting fires.

The idea of fire insurance was first introduced in 1240. In Flanders, a community-wide fire insurance pool was developed that reimbursed the losses of an individual from the resources of the others. This concept also gave great emphasis to fire prevention because the losses were personally felt by everyone.

At that time the only fire fighting tools were the bucket brigade and simple wooden ladders. With the rise and fall of the Greek and Roman empires, the techniques created by Hero were lost. While Hero had developed a means of squirting water on the fire, firefighters of the 900s through 1200s had to improvise with nothing more than leather buckets. Their method was very ineffective, especially if a fire got large.

Even Marco Polo paid attention to the problem of fire. During his travels in China, he wrote about a "civil force of watchmen" who traveled the streets of Chinese cities at night looking for unfriendly fires.

The major cities of Europe were often ravaged by fire. London and Paris were partially destroyed several times. In the 1400s, during an invasion by the Tartars, fire was used as a weapon of war. Reportedly two hundred thousand people lost their lives in the widespread fires that resulted from the warfare.

It eventually became obvious to European merchants and leaders that something had to be done to cope with the problem. In

1518 an anonymous individual resurrected the idea of the pump-syringe that Hero had developed three thousand years before. In 1566 London lawmakers passed a law that limited the fuel a baker could store next to the oven, and in 1583 Parliament forbade tallow chandlers (candle makers) to melt tallow in dwellings.

The fire service in Europe thus had become very conscious of fire prevention. The fire service in Europe gradually developed combat capability through the use of the armed forces. The Paris Fire Brigade is a division of the French army. Much of this heritage lives on in the professional fire service in Europe today. The American fire service took a different path from the European approach, when many political and social changes occurred on both continents in the 1600s and 1700s.

## Early America

In the early 1600s, many European explorers were making their first settlements in the New World. The ability to fight fire was still limited, so fire was a real threat to the early colonists. One of the colonies, Jamestown, burned in 1610, and the colony was abandoned for a while. Leaders in the infant colonies were terrorized to hear the word "fire." When a dwelling burned in that era, it often had catastrophic effects, especially if the fire occurred in the harsh New England winter.

Of course, pioneers who had braved the Atlantic Ocean were not going to give up easily. It became extremely important to these settlers that they protect their property. As early as 1631, lawmakers in the cities of Boston and New Amsterdam (now New York City) passed laws prohibiting such things as thatched roofs and wooden chimneys. (That's right—*wooden* chimneys! The colonists made them of planks and coated them with clay. Needless to say, they often caught fire.)

The new laws did not keep the colonies from suffering disaster. A fire that got close enough to ignite eighteen barrels of gunpowder destroyed a major portion of Boston in 1645.

The problem of fire would simply not go away from the newly founded cities and towns. The idea of fire prevention was a sound one and was followed as closely as possible. But the new cities were growing rapidly, and the people who populated the early communities were rugged individualists who had come to the New World to get away from laws and regulations. Some of the new fire prevention laws were simply ignored, so stringent enforcement by the authorities became necessary.

New Amsterdam took the issue on directly in 1647 and appointed some surveyors of buildings. Their job was to check the construction of new buildings against the code. The surveyors were supplemented in 1648 by another group called fire wardens. Their job was to inspect for conditions that could breed fire.

For almost one hundred years, the emphasis was on fire prevention. People at that time seemed to feel that uncontrolled fires were a great liability and that they were best dealt with by not having them. Benjamin Franklin's slogan "An ounce of prevention is worth a pound of cure" was actually the first fire prevention message.

## Volunteers

During the colonial period, all fire fighting was done by a volunteer system. Everyone was a firefighter when the town bells rang. In 1653 Boston passed a law that required each residence to own a bucket, a ladder that would reach the ridge pole of the roof, a twelve-foot pole with a swab on the end, and ropes and hooks for pulling down a burning house. But the problem of fire got continually worse.

The reasons for the increased fire problem were complex. The American colonies originally were merely outposts of European countries. The cities and towns were engaged in the enterprise of growing, producing, and shipping products to the king of a far-away country. Warehousing was a common enterprise. Population centers tended to be crowded into small, congested areas.

It is interesting to compare the Boston or New York of today to the cities of the early 1600s in this respect. These cities were very vulnerable to fire then, as they are today, because of the problems of overcrowding and combustible construction. Early American homes were built mostly of wood and were very flammable.

Boston was among the first to take some aggressive actions against fire. First, the council ordered a Jynks Fire Injine from England in the early 1700s. Then they instituted the bellmen, who patrolled the streets from 10:00 P.M. until 5:00 A.M. looking for fire. It quickly became clear that when the bells were rung, everyone paid attention, so the bellmen were extended to an around-the-clock basis.

In the last part of the 1600s, Boston was again almost destroyed by fire. The city council authorized the formation of the volunteers of the city into groups of similar background so that they could fight fire more effectively. This was probably the first formal attempt to create a fire department.

## *Fire Insurance and Early Stations*

Fire insurance arrived in the New World in 1736 when a firm started the concept in South Carolina. The practice did not take hold, however, because community after community lacked an effective way of dealing with fires after they started.

One of the first individuals to recognize this deficiency and then attempt to do something about it was a historical figure better known for his political views—Benjamin Franklin. In the 1730s Franklin decided to join the concepts of prevention and protection so that the insurance industry would have a reasonable expectation of a profit. Franklin established some of the first truly organized fire brigades in Philadelphia. Much of his writing in *Poor Richard's Almanac* was directed toward fire prevention measures.

Franklin's insurance company was among the first to use the idea of fire marks in America. Fire marks were molded lead symbols that were put up on the outside of homes to tell the responding volunteer firefighters which insurance company would be responsible to repay the losses. Today these insurance fire marks are still to be seen in some restored areas of the early colonial era. In the city of Alexandria, Virginia, you can still see fire marks on the buildings right down the street from George Washington's fire station—Friendship Engine Company #1.

While Franklin was busy developing the idea of fire prevention and insurance, other men such as George Washington and Thomas Jefferson supported the building of fire stations to house the infant fire departments. John Hancock purchased a fire apparatus and donated it to the city of Boston. It was named Hancock Engine Company #10 and saw service for many years. The period just before the American Revolution was probably when the combat aspects of fire service began to separate from the prevention aspects.

Fire stations in the early days were almost entirely structured around social, economic, or racial conformity. Because volunteers staffed the fire stations, membership in a company was considered a privilege.

## Hand Pumpers and Bucket Brigades

By the end of the 1700s, technology was rapidly replacing the bucket brigade. A reciprocating pump that operated out of a tub-like affair had been developed in England. The design concepts of the modern fire pumper have an obscure beginning in the makings of the Newsham hand pumper that was in service at that time. At first, pumpers could only put out a very limited amount of water. Nozzles were affixed to the top of the pump, so it had to be right next to the fire to do any good.

Nonetheless, these mechanical changes affected the way that fire departments were organized. The obligation of every citizen to join the fire bucket brigade gave way to the formation of the volunteer fire company. The formation of the fire companies gave rise to the development of institutions to manage and control them.

The fire apparatus became a focal point of the organization. Because the departments had nothing else on which to spend their money or time, the fire engine was often an object of great expense. A visit to any fire museum will demonstrate this fact. Some of the pieces of equipment were gold-leafed and wildly ornate.

Membership in the volunteer fire company was most often on the basis of popularity or compatibility with the group. There were Irish fire companies, usually with the word *Hibernia* in the title. There was a company called the African Fire Company located in Philadelphia that consisted entirely of African-Americans.

Leadership in these organizations was given to people on the basis of popularity. One such individual, Jacobus Stoutenburgh, a gunsmith, was appointed as the overseer of fire engines by his company. Later on his official title was changed to *engenier*. Still later it was changed to *chief engineer*, a title that is still used today for the officer in charge of a fire department.

One of the most easily recognized of all American institutions was also developed in the 1700s—the American fire helmet. The first fire helmets looked a lot like stovepipe hats. They were not distinctive. In the late 1700s, a leather craftsman named Andrew Gratacap built a helmet that had a high peaked dome, a short brim on the front, and a long brim in the back to shed water and debris. The large, often decorative frontispiece that was added to this helmet was taken from the hats of the German Hessian soldiers who came to fight in the Revolutionary War. Gratacap took the idea and painted names and numbers on the piece. This practice is still in vogue in many places.

## Involvement in War

Few people realized that these volunteer fire companies, because of their political involvement, were part of the drama of the Revolutionary War. The famous, or perhaps infamous, Boston Massacre resulted after a large crowd had gathered on a commons after someone had rung the fire bells in a false alarm. One of the victims of that incident was a Boston volunteer firefighter.

Once the war started, fire was even used as a weapon against the British. As American forces retreated in some areas, they practiced what is called the *scorched-earth policy*. This meant that they burned everything that might help the enemy in the captured area. Unfortunately, that practice was to return to haunt the country in the War of 1812 and in the Civil War.

From the early 1800s on, the separate institutions of the fire service began to develop on different tracks. The fire insurance industry focused on the economics of the fire problem. The fire fighting element focused on the development of equipment and hardware to combat fires as well as social and organizational relationships to manage the personnel involved. Fire prevention waned during this entire period.

## *Improved Water Systems*

Technology did not stop, however. Boston installed a water main system in the early 1800s, and water systems began to be an important part of the fire fighting team. Most of the early mains were nothing more than hollowed-out logs that were bonded together. Firefighters got to the water by digging up the main and chopping a hole in the log. The hole was replaced later by a stake or post. Frequently the posts or stakes were left rising up from the dirt so that if fire companies had to fight a fire in the same area again, all they had to do was to pull out the plug and they had water. We still call fire hydrants *plugs*, even though they don't actually plug anything.

The development of water systems and the developing Industrial Revolution both gave a boost to the fire protection field. In just twenty-five years, the fire hose was invented, fire hydrants were built on water mains, and the hand pumper was invented. (It was a very large hand pumper and took thirty to sixty men to operate it.)

During that same era, the country was very severely damaged by fire. The British destroyed Washington, D.C., by fire, during the War of 1812. New York was devastated by a great fire on December 16 and 17, 1835. Volunteer fire companies became more and more needed, and at the same time they became more politically powerful.

As pride in the volunteers grew, so did the problems of managing the fire companies. The different companies began to wear different types of uniforms. The technology that created the Philadelphia pumper had helped create a system long on human resources but limited on control.

Some of the early leaders in the fire service took the responsibility seriously. "Uncle Tommy" Franklin of the New York volunteer companies was a man who never abused his position over his men. "Handsome Jim" Gulick followed Uncle Tommy without repercussions. From 1830 to 1850, leaders of the volunteer companies used the position to achieve political office. "Boss" Tweed, who was later indicted for corruption in the Tammany Hall scandal, was a foreman of a volunteer fire company that followed this path.

Political intrigue and the mixture of politics, rum, and rowdiness in the firehouse came to a head in Cincinnati in the 1850s. Several volunteer fire companies responded to a fire in that city and spent so much time fighting with each other that they didn't fight the fire. Because the different insurance companies often reimbursed only the fire company that fought a fire first, there was always rivalry over who was the first to arrive. Many fires got out of control while volunteer companies decided that issue with their fists. This time the building burned to the ground. Cincinnati city officials, irate at the action, decided to replace their volunteers with something else.

## Paid Firefighters

The "something else" that they chose was a paid professional fire department. Because the large hand-operated pumpers required so much physical effort to use, the city leaders in Cincinnati decided to try a steam-powered fire pumper, which was newly invented by John Ericsson (who later designed the Federal iron-sided boat the *Monitor* that fought in the Civil War). They contracted with Moses Latta to build the steamer, and he delivered the pumper in 1854.

William Channing, a doctor, developed a telegraph fire alarm system at about the same time. The die was cast. Although volunteers had served the cities, towns, and villages for decades, something was going to change. Unfortunately, there was also a big change on the horizon for the entire country—the Civil War.

## Civil War Fire Problems

Typically, one of the first groups to volunteer to fight in the war was the volunteer firefighters. On April 27, 1861, the Fire Zouaves were formed from a group of New York firefighters. Colonel John Ellsworth, their commanding officer, was the first Union officer killed in the war. He was shot and killed in Alexandria, Virginia, within a rock's throw of the Friendship Engine Company.

After three months of that conflict, only 380 of the original 1,000 Fire Zouaves were still alive. Today, in some decorator shops, you can see a wooden plaque that shows a firefighter wearing his helmet and carrying a hose that is inscribed First in Peace, First in War. In a way, that is a tribute to the courage and conviction of the volunteer firefighters of that era.

The war caused its own kind of fire problems. In New York, the draft riots resulted in fires that killed and injured many people. New York still had volunteers on the job at that time, and there was a lot of pressure on those who had remained behind.

Sherman practiced the scorched-earth policy on his march toward Atlanta. This act, which was immortalized in the book and movie *Gone with the Wind*, was one of the most graphic demonstrations of the awesome and terrible aspects of fire used as a weapon of war.

The volunteers continued to serve. In 1865 the famous P. T. Barnum Museum burned to the ground, destroying thousands of artifacts and memorabilia. The time had come to replace the volunteer firefighter in the large cities. Returning war veterans, many without any source of income, were given an opportunity to serve in a new role—the paid firefighter.

This did not totally mean the end of volunteerism. Even today there are hundreds of thousands of volunteer firefighters serving their communities. However, as many communities grow from small to large, the pressure to create a paid fire department increases. The increase in the number of alarms and the complexity of fire protection often causes volunteer systems to change to paid or partially paid forces.

Interestingly, the fact that so many veterans joined the fire services is still being felt today. For example, most fire departments use variations of blue in their uniforms, and company officers are usually called *captain* or *lieutenant*. Both of these ranks appear to be holdovers from the military. Upper-grade officers are referred to as *battalion chiefs*, another reference to military organization. Most fire fighting agencies are structured in a semimilitary fashion.

## Horse-Drawn Pumpers

There was one big problem. As paid forces began to pick up the responsibility to handle the combat aspects of fire fighting, they realized that they needed help. Steam fire apparatus replaced the large number of volunteers used to pump the water. The only problem was that steam fire pumpers weighed about ten tons. The solution was to employ horses to draw the apparatus.

If there was any one period in which the fire service gained the most in the way of image, it was during the horse-drawn era. A team of matched horses at the gallop, pulling a smoke-belching steamer over brick streets, was a delight of sight and sound. Unfortunately, it did little to slow down the devastation of business and industry by fire.

On October 6, 1871, as the story goes, Mrs. O'Leary's cow kicked over a lantern in a Chicago barn and started the most-often-cited conflagration in the history of the United States. More than eighteen hundred buildings burned, and three hundred people lost their lives. The Great Chicago Fire serves as the anniversary date for the annual National Fire Prevention Week. On the same date, a major brushfire rushed through Peshtigo, a small Wisconsin town. In that fire, twelve hundred people lost their lives.

## Fire Protection Engineering

In the late 1800s, the arsenal against fire was awesome, but it was a losing battle. The textile mill industry was being hit very hard. Henry S. Parmalee, an enterprising young man, invented the automatic fire sprinkler. This device holds water back in a water piping system until a solder link melts and lets the water out on the fire. Parmalee's efforts resulted in the development of a whole new field of fire protection—fire protection engineering.

In about a decade, several other inventions resulted from the marriage of manual fire fighting techniques and the insight of the engineer. Fire alarm systems were expanded, and water systems were analyzed from the standpoint of hydraulics. Some of the work accomplished by early engineers like John Freeman is still used as the foundation of fire protection engineering.

In quick succession, a firefighter invented the first aerial ladder and the firehouse pole to get out of the station more quickly. The first poles were not made of brass; they were made of polished wood.

The turn of the century did not bring the solution to the fire problem, either. In 1903 there was a tremendous fire in Chicago's Iroquois Theatre that killed 575 people. In 1904 the city of Baltimore was swept by a conflagration.

In the insurance industry, a nationwide system called the National Board of Fire Underwriters was formed. Eventually this organization became the American Insurance Association and then the Insurance Service Office. The relationship between good fire protection and insurance losses was rebuilt. This relationship, although it changes from time to time, especially as the economy rises and falls, forms the basis for many fire protection careers.

On April 18, 1906, the city of San Francisco was jolted by an earthquake that sparked numerous fires. For several days San Francisco firefighters waged a block-by-block, house-by-house battle to save the city. Although seven hundred people died, the only firefighter to lose his life in that fire was the chief. He was killed when his own home collapsed. Not one of the city's thirty-eight engine companies went out of service that day.

## Motorized Fire Fighting Vehicles

Even as motorized apparatus replaced the horses in the fire station, catastrophic losses still occurred. In 1911 a fire occurred in New York's Triangle Shirtwaist Factory, and 143 employees died. Some of the equipment that responded to that terrible loss was powered by horses and some by motorcar. Although technology was changing, fires were not any easier to stop.

As the horses were being replaced, the very same firefighters who had replaced the volunteers were the ones who resisted the changes represented by the new automotive apparatus. Their resistance to the change from horses to horsepower was natural, but it did not prevent the change.

One of the most important fires that occurred to reverse the fire service's attitude about one of its basic functions was Boston's Cocoanut Grove fire in 1942. This fire, which resulted in the death of 492 people and injury to 181 others, caused fire officials to look at the problems of building construction, exit requirements, building materials, and building conditions that can endanger occupants. The whole idea of fire prevention as an important element of fire protection began to reestablish itself.

Major fire losses have continued to occur despite this effort. In 1953 a fire in a General Motors factory resulted in a $35 million loss. In the 1960s a brushfire raging through the Bel Air and Malibu areas of Los Angeles destroyed hundreds of homes and businesses. Major losses of the 1970s included the Beverly Hills Supper Club fire in Kentucky.

In the 1980s the fire service experienced major high-rise fires, such as the First Interstate Bank Building in Los Angeles. Hazardous materials incidents such as the Kansas City ammonium nitrate explosion and the Henderson, Nevada, rocket fuel fire resulted in catastrophic losses. In 1993 the city of Oakland, California, experienced one of the largest losses—millions of dollars of property and the lives of both firefighters and civilians—in the history of the United States. The "urban-wildland fire" has continued to grow in significance over the last ten years. Once a phenomena of the western United States, urban-wildland fires now strike in areas all over the country from Florida to Maine and from the Carolinas to Washington. The attack upon the World Trade Center on September 11, 2001, resulted in the largest single loss of life to the American fire service in its entire history; 343 firefighters died on that day trying to assist people in evacuating the Twin Towers.

## Modern Fire Protection

Fire protection has grown into a multibillion-dollar industry in this country. So far in this chapter we have discussed the historical precedent in four major occupational areas that deal with the nation's fire problem: fire prevention, fire protection engineering, fire insurance, and fire suppression or fire fighting forces. Each of these fields is growing and changing, and from these fundamental areas, new areas of specialization develop and spawn yet others every day.

In the late 1960s President Richard Nixon created a National Commission on Fire Prevention and Control. This commission published a book entitled *America Burning*. As a result of that book, the federal government formed the National Fire Protection and Control Administration (NFPCA). Under President Carter the name was changed to the U.S. Fire Administration. The U.S. Fire Administration funded many programs that have helped the fire service, such as the National Fire Data Center and the National Fire Academy. Even though this federal agency made an attempt to deal with the nationwide fire problem, it is still apparent that solutions to the fire problem are neither simple nor final. *America Burning, Recommissioned* was created during the Clinton administration to refocus our attention on the continuation of the nation's fire problem. It reinforced the fact that although valiant efforts have been made to change the problem, it continues to grow.

In the 1980s we saw significant improvements in fire protection with the installation of automatic fire sprinklers and more smoke detectors. Additionally, fire departments were given an expanded role in dealing with emergency medical services and public education in many communities. At the same time, however, major losses of life occurred due to fires such as the Las Vegas MGM Grand Hotel fire and the First Interstate Bank Building. There was also a tremendous increase in amount and use of hazardous materials and an almost epidemic arson problem.

We have come a long way from turning buckets into fire fighting tools. We have expanded our knowledge of fire but failed to gain complete control over it. We have increased our sophistication in equipment, methods, and techniques, yet we still have catastrophic losses. With the increased demands of society, a greater responsibility is placed on those who choose the fire protection field. As society and technology change, the fire problem changes, and the fire protection field has to keep pace.

The fire service has learned something from every major loss in the past. We call that the "catastrophic theory of reform." Out of the Iroquois Theatre fire came new standards for drapes and curtains in public auditoriums; out of the Cocoanut Grove fire came standards for exits that open in the direction of the occupants escaping. The challenge the fire protection field faces is that there is always some problem without an existing solution.

This phenomenon has continued in the fire service through the turn of the century. For example, starting with the Oakland conflagration in the mid-1990s, we have seen a new emphasis on dealing with conflagration-type fires—something that we had thought was a part of the past. In 1993 a series of devastating fires destroyed parts of Laguna Beach and Malibu, California. Then a major urban-wildland fire impacted Long Island, New York. The problem, which has been labeled the "Urban-Wildland Interface," is very much a part of the changing nature of the fire problem in the United States. Just when the fire service thinks that it has resolved a significant part of its problem, a new one emerges.

The two largest areas of growth in the last two decades of the fire service have been the field of emergency medical services (EMS) and hazardous materials response. Both of these areas of responsibility have been accepted by many fire agencies as a natural extension of their basic mission of protecting life and property. This adaptation is not universal. There are still fire agencies that do not wish to be tasked with these programs. The trend, however, is for more and more departments to accept this expanded role.

Another area that has seen considerable growth is the role of fire agencies in response to disasters. In the last few decades we have witnessed major events, such as the Loma Prieta and Northridge, California, earthquakes in the West; the massive wind damage events in the Southeast; floods in the Midwest; and the impact of man-made disasters such as the bombing of both the federal building in Oklahoma City and the high-rise in New York City or the air accidents that occurred in Washington, D.C., and Florida.

As a result of these two trends there has been considerable interest in specialization in the fire service and the creation of highly sophisticated teams to respond to these catastrophic events. Specialization has taken the form of creating some vertical career alignment around a field of technology that is independent of the organizational rank structure. For example, individuals entering the EMS field may move from first responder (minimum training and education) through qualified paramedic (extensive training and education), and yet never change rank in the fire service. The same could be said for members of hazardous materials (HAZ-MAT) or search and rescue (USAR) teams that become specialists and technicians independent of their day-to-day rank.

The future of the fire service contains many more opportunities for change. Advances in technology used in our everyday lives will be part of the change for the fire service, too. Information technology, linked with the complexity of contemporary life, will create some new capabilities for emergency services workers. Tools such as Global Positioning Systems (GPS) or Geographic Information Systems (GIS) will be part of the tools of the trade for fire service professionals. Computers, which are now almost universal in their availability, will evolve into tools that will be used for everything from operating built-in fire protection systems to providing on-scene decision support for fire officers.

The next few years will also see an increase in diversity in the workforce. Although this change had its origins in the recent past, demographic shifts and greater awareness of the value that diversity brings to the workforce will cause opportunities to increase for candidates from different gender and ethnic backgrounds.

## Summary

The mission of the fire service is to protect life and property. We no longer have fire laws that deal with thatched roofs or candle-making in the house, but the type of people who select the fire profession as a career has never really changed. They are people who want to protect lives and property and serve their fellow human beings.

# 2

# The Fire Protection Field

IF YOU ASK the average person to describe what a firefighter does, he or she will probably describe the job of the municipal firefighter. A common image for the fire service is that of a fire truck with a red light flashing and siren wailing as it rolls down the street. That is the public perception of fire protection. But the fire service is much more complex and sophisticated than that.

The fire service is an occupation that is rich in heritage and tradition. In this chapter we will explore both traditional and non-traditional jobs in fire service. We will look at a wide range of careers that may or may not ever involve the task of physically fighting fire. The fire service has career opportunities for men and women, for the physically fit and the disabled, for those of normal intelligence and the engineering genius. The only prerequisite is a desire to serve humankind by dedicating one's life to the protection of life and property. There are hundreds of different ways in which that can be accomplished.

The jobs we will discuss in this chapter are typical of the different opportunities that exist within the framework of the four basic fire service career paths: fire suppression, fire prevention, fire engineering, and fire insurance. An added element will be the discussion of these job opportunities as they exist within the public (or governmental) and private sectors.

Basically, we will identify only the entry-level occupations that are typical of these areas. The jobs we will describe are not all-inclusive, but rather a sampling of the types of job descriptions that a person might find in reviewing job flyers or announcements.

## A Changing Profession—Public or Private

Most entry-level jobs available in fire protection are found in the different levels of the government: local, regional, state, or federal. A smaller number of jobs are available in the private sector. That may change in the future. Most of the positions described here are civil service jobs. Actual job titles, hiring requirements, and specific details will be established by city, county, state, or federal government personnel systems. Descriptions in this chapter are general in nature, have been obtained from a variety of sources, and are a combination of actual descriptions.

You will have to do some follow-up research on the descriptions to get a complete picture of the jobs described. There is another reason you should read as much specific information as possible on the jobs: they are changing as society and technology change. The information given here is as correct as it can be for now, but the evolutionary process described in the first chapter is still in motion.

Many different jobs that may be available are described here, but they are not all equally available. Openings in some jobs are frequent, with high turnover rates; other jobs are stable and do not grow very rapidly. If a particular job interests you, it is important that you carry out research to gather specific details.

But don't be discouraged. Absolute numbers of fire protection jobs will continually increase through the next few decades. What may change are the mix of private versus public fire protection opportunities and the ratio of positions at the local, regional, state, and federal levels. The educational and minimum qualifications for the various positions are also likely to change. They will probably become more rigid in some areas and relax in others.

## Competition

Another factor that bears serious consideration in the evaluation of fire service jobs is competition. The number of candidates for many of these jobs is very high, and the number of entry-level positions is very low. Preparation is the key to success in obtaining any of these jobs. As you read through the various jobs, you will note a wide range of skills, aptitudes, knowledge, and educational requirements.

We should caution that the fairly low entry-level requirements are no indication of requirements for promotion in the various fields. A good example is the firefighter job. While the entry-level requirements of this position are not nearly as high as they are for some other positions, the requirements for promotion become more extensive each day.

The characteristics that would make a person a good candidate for each of these jobs are called "worker traits." In as many cases as possible, we mention the worker traits of these jobs as a guide for you to explore further. This information can be of assistance in discussion with a counselor or with a person in a fire service job you are looking into. Don't ignore clues that these worker traits provide. They are very important in predicting potential success, especially as it relates to entry-level jobs. These traits are derived from studies that have been conducted to determine the minimum performance required on a job.

It helps to start with the obvious because it is the most familiar. So we will start off with the basic entry-level position for the field called public fire protection. Typically, this job would be called firefighter.

## Local Fire Departments

Local government supplies most of the fire protection services provided in the United States and Canada. Most communities have a fire department that provides the basic resources. Typically this consists of fire stations, fire apparatus, and personnel assigned to respond on that equipment. If you are looking at the fire service as a possible career, this may be the place to start to evaluate the job opportunities.

The entry-level job most common to fire departments is the probationary (or rookie) firefighter. When anyone becomes a member of a fire department, he or she is usually required to go through extensive training for the first six months to see if he or she has the characteristics and ability to do the job of fire fighting. Probationary firefighters are typically required to complete a combination of classroom and field training, to demonstrate their ability to learn the range of topics required of a firefighter, and to prove that they can perform the physical labor of the job.

## *Entry Requirements*

Most fire departments do not have pretraining requirements for the entry-level firefighter. In the majority of the cities, counties, and regional governments that provide fire protection, the only educational requirement is a high school diploma. In some areas community colleges are providing pre-entry training, and although it is definitely a plus to have completed the training, it is not required. This does not imply that the knowledge level tested for is low. On the contrary, most fire examinations cannot be successfully passed unless the individual has a good basic education in math and English.

Individuals selected for entry into fire departments at this level are carefully screened to see if they possess the mental capacity to understand things such as fire chemistry and behavior, fluid hydraulics, electricity, and building construction. The physical demands include being able to carry heavy weight, agility to move about with equipment, the absence of fear of heights or enclosures, and personal ability to get along in a teamwork atmosphere.

## *Probation*

Because fire departments are usually organized in a paramilitary structure, probationary firefighters are expected to prove themselves in a variety of conditions, from the classroom to action under emergency conditions.

Entry level in the fire department focuses a great deal on two very important areas of fire fighting: discipline and knowledge of tools and equipment. The former is required to allow command and control of personnel when they are involved in serious emergencies. The latter is required to put the equipment into service during emergencies.

Probation periods can be as short as six months or as long as eighteen months, depending upon the needs and type of fire department. Generally the probation period is about one year. Completion of the probation period often requires a combination of time on the job, completion of examinations, and a satisfactory grade from the supervisor.

At the end of the probationary period, the firefighter is eligible to continue up the career ladder of the department. Depending upon the size and complexity of the department, that can range from a few simple promotional opportunities to a veritable kaleidoscope of occupational specialties.

## Promotion Possibilities

If one chooses to remain in the combat arm of the fire service, the promotions are based on different levels of responsibility. A firefighter can become an apparatus operator (the driver of the fire truck), then a company commander, then a chief officer. One can also move into a field of specialization such as emergency medical technician (EMT), paramedic, or hazardous material technician (HMT), or be involved in aircraft crash rescue; harbor or waterfront fire fighting; training, maintenance, and fire inspection; or arson investigation.

Each specialization has educational and experience requirements that are somewhat unique to that field. The knowledge that is required to make a good training officer in a fire department is very different from the knowledge required of a good arson investigator.

Generally, however, the entry-level firefighter does not have to worry about that. The decision to select one or more of the fields of specialization is not made until the entry-level firefighter has completed probation. In actual practice, few people make the choice until they have been on the job for several years. After completing the basic training for the field, the rest of the education and training requirements for the fields of specialization become self-apparent.

In Chapter 9 we will examine promotional opportunities and discuss the various career ladders that you might pursue.

## *Other Entry-Level Opportunities*

An important factor not to be ignored is that many fire departments are beginning to "civilianize" many functions formerly performed by uniformed firefighters. The field of fire prevention, for instance, used to be staffed only by people who had served in suppression roles and were transferred because of injury or some other problem. That is no longer the case.

### Fire Inspector

Fire prevention inspector is not the same type of job as that of the firefighter. In a fire prevention bureau, people perform tasks such as plan checks of buildings before they are constructed and make technical inspections of hazardous materials installations. The job entails going out to places of business and public assemblage to check on code requirements. It often involves issuing violation notices to property owners to get them to bring their property up to the fire code requirements. The job of the fire inspector is not physically demanding, it is mentally demanding.

Because fire inspectors are dealing with a very specific field of knowledge, they need different skills. Among these skills are the ability to work with the public, to perform in-depth analyses, and to write well. Knowledge of the law, hazardous materials, and inspection techniques are also important to an inspector. Actual fire fighting experience is not a necessity for this type of work.

For that reason, many fire departments are now opening up entry-level positions in the fire prevention bureaus. Unlike entry-level fire fighting jobs, entry-level inspector positions often require some pretraining. Typically, these jobs require a college education, usually in the field of fire sciences.

## Public Fire Educator

Another area in which the fire service seems to be changing is the field of public education. This field of specialization stems from the fire prevention area. It involves working with individuals and groups to inform them of fire safety practices in the home and at work.

This job does not require physical strength either. It is a job that uses public speaking skills, knowledge of instructional techniques, audiovisual materials, and an ability to plan, organize, and deliver programs to all age groups.

Educational requirements for public fire education are not clearly defined at this time because the job is relatively new to fire service. Generally, people working in this area have backgrounds in either education or public relations. Some have a background in journalism or the media. In almost all cases, the jobs require some form of college education accompanied by experience in working with people.

## Fire Apparatus Mechanic

In the larger cities, fire departments also have positions in the field of apparatus maintenance, but these are rarely filled from the entry level. Most apparatus mechanics have developed their skills in another area and transferred into fire department openings. These technicians have usually received training in trade or technical schools.

## Dispatcher and Communications

Another position available at the entry level in most fire agencies is the dispatcher or communications job. This job entails answering the emergency telephone and sending out fire trucks to the scene of an emergency. It often involves the use of a wide variety of electronic devices, including radios, alarms, computers, and testing equipment.

The dispatcher position is not physically demanding, but it is among the most difficult mentally. The job requires remembering complex dispatch procedures, memorizing radio procedures, and making decisions involving the nature of emergencies and the proper equipment to be dispatched. In addition, much emphasis is placed on the accuracy of information relayed to the fire units in the field. A great deal of the time is taken up with paperwork and writing reports.

One of the problems with the dispatcher position is that it seldom has a career ladder associated with it. An individual often has to go out of the communications field to achieve promotion and pay raises of any magnitude. On the other hand, many a young firefighter has gotten a foot in the door by putting in time as a dispatcher. As a matter of fact, many departments use the dispatcher position as an internship to the position of probationary firefighter.

## Clerical and Secretarial Jobs

The last entry-level job that might be available in a local fire department would be as a clerk or secretary. Almost all fire departments have positions that serve the administration, the fire prevention bureaus, the training staff, and the fire chief's office.

On the surface, these positions do not appear any different from similar jobs in other fields. There is a subtle difference, however.

Clerical and secretarial personnel in the fire service have greater than average contact with the public they serve, and the jobs usually involve a great deal of personal responsibility. Frequently, the clerical staff gets involved in the same programs that the fire personnel are involved in managing.

Of course, keying is keying and filing is filing. But the nature of the fire service is such that the clerk or secretary may be keying a training manual one minute and an arson investigation report the next. Many people who started as clerical staff have gone on to positions in the fire prevention bureaus and public education staffs.

## State Forestry Job Opportunities

Few local fire departments have extensive forestry fire fighting positions because the wildland fire problem is usually considered a state or federal responsibility. In some areas, especially in the western and southeastern part of the United States, forestry is also a responsibility of the county governments by contract with the state government.

### Seasonal Jobs

Because of the nature of the seasons, forestry or wildland fire fighting is not normally a year-round job. In most cases, the entry-level positions are seasonal—the positions are only open when the fire season is in effect. The fire season is normally from the beginning of summer through Labor Day. In some areas, it may continue until the first rains of the winter.

Seasonal fire fighting is one of the best ways of learning the basics of fire control and getting a look at the nature of fire fighting. A seasonal firefighter will find that most of the work is simple, hard, manual labor. Most wildland fires are fought with axes and shovels to cut down brush and timber from the path of the fire. The job often involves using saws and sometimes heavy equipment like bulldozers.

In some areas, the forestry firefighter gets the opportunity to respond on fire apparatus designed especially for off-the-road operations. Working on these pumpers often means laying long hose up hills or down ridges to get to a fire. Even being assigned to the pumper does not relieve the forestry firefighter of the duty of cutting fire breaks, overhauling burned-over areas, and engaging in the manual labor aspect of the job.

The job will usually have very minimal entrance requirements because its wages are low and turnover is high. The most common requirements are to be physically fit, be of the age of majority (usually eighteen), and possess a good work record. The emphasis is on physical conditioning.

The number of professional firefighters who got their start in this fashion is very high, especially in the states with severe forestry fire problems. It is a good job for the student considering a fire service profession: it is seasonal, which fits the usual academic calendar; it is intense, which gives a person a sense of whether he or she likes fire fighting; and it is rewarding.

But the job of forestry fire fighting is not all glamour. When forestry fire personnel are not on fires, they spend a great deal of their time working on mundane jobs like trail and building maintenance and preparing equipment for the time when fire does strike. And it has become increasingly dangerous. Firefighters suffered casualties in several major fires in the last ten years involving wildland fires. Events such as the Storm King fire in Colorado and the Thirty Mile fire in Oregon have focused attention on the danger in these types of jobs.

## Promotional Opportunities

Promotional opportunities in the forest fire area are directly dependent on success over several years as a seasonal firefighter. In most of the states and in the federal fire service, a person can get into a permanent full-time job only by competing against others with seasonal experience. Full-time jobs in the forestry area are more difficult to obtain than full-time positions in urban fire departments. In addition, these full-time jobs are very demanding on one's family and social life.

After permanent appointment in these jobs, one must be willing to accept the fact that transfers from one area to another may occur and that there will be long periods away from the family. Much of the work of the forestry firefighter is in remote areas, and the fires they are involved in often take many days, even weeks, to control. For example, the fire season of 2001 kept workers in the western United States busy for most of the summer, as fire devoured thousands of acres of forests that ignited more easily than usual as a result of widespread drought conditions.

## Federal Fire Departments

The United States government is one of the largest employers of individuals in the business of fire protection. Job opportunities there fall into several categories: military fire protection, forestry fire protection (an extension of the previous section, but on a federal level), fire protection for special facilities, fire protection engineering, and specialized fire protection programs.

## Military Fire Protection

The United States Department of Defense operates a large fire protection program that includes everything from aircraft fire rescue to structural fire protection for bases all around the world. Many young people interested in entering the fire protection field have gotten their basic training by joining the military and going to the respective schools operated by the various branches of the military. The U.S. Air Force maintains training in the specialized field of crash-fire rescue (CFR). This is the type of fire fighting done to protect aircraft when accidents occur, primarily during take-off and landing.

The U.S. Navy has fire fighting specialists, too. Most of the training in the navy concentrates on the problem of controlling fire aboard ships. It is often referred to as damage control instead of fire fighting, but the training is similar. Such fire fighting training played a key role in containing the blaze that erupted aboard the USS *Iowa* in 1989 following an explosion in one of the battleship's gun turrets. Though the disaster claimed forty-seven lives, casualties and damage could have been much worse without firefighters to keep the flames under control. One can also get training in aircraft fire rescue in the navy.

Most entry-level jobs in military fire protection are designed for the initial enlistment trainee and do not provide much promotional opportunity. Many military bases have fire departments with both military and civilian fire personnel.

The requirements for military fire service are similar to the entry-level requirements for a municipal fire department. The job is both physically and mentally demanding, so the criteria are close to the same as for any fire department. This is good for the trainee because success in military training indicates possible success in a civilian job upon completion of the enlistment.

Many military bases have fire departments that closely resemble their neighboring cities. Because the military organizations have a high turnover, the structural protection for most bases is left in the hands of a fire department that does not have to be transferred with a specific unit. Customarily, a civilian fire officer commands these departments, but he or she reports to a military commander.

## Federal Forestry Fire Protection

The federal government maintains a large contingent of forestry firefighters. The three largest agencies are the U.S. Forest Service, the U.S. Park Service, and the Bureau of Land Management. These three agencies employ a large number of both seasonal and permanent employees.

The U.S. Forest Service protects the areas of the country that are called national forests. These are primarily areas that have been set aside to protect national resources like timber, mining, and watershed. There are national forests in almost all of the fifty states. The agency is part of the Department of Agriculture; it is charged with protecting the nation's natural resources from fire. During any given year, the U.S. Forest Service may fight hundreds of thousands of fires that are caused by either human carelessness or the natural elements, such as lightning.

The U.S. Park Service is a division of the Department of the Interior; it is charged with the task of protecting the national parks. These are primarily areas that have been set aside for recreational purposes. One of the interesting aspects of the U.S. Park Service responsibilities is that people in the entry-level positions often get involved in very complex mountain rescues and some law enforcement activities.

The Bureau of Land Management (BLM) is also part of the Department of the Interior; it is charged with the responsibility to protect the large land areas that are under federal ownership but not classified as parks or forests. These areas are primarily wide, open rangeland or areas where property is still available for homesteading. The BLM is an interesting fire fighting agency in that it has an extremely diverse inventory of fire fighting equipment. As a result of its involvement in range fires, for example, it has developed very specialized apparatus.

The Department of Interior also has fire personnel involved in the Bureau of Indian Affairs. These firefighters are responsible to provide protection on reservations. This involves both structural and watershed fire protection.

All of the agencies mentioned in this section have standards for employment that emphasize physical and mental capabilities. The type of work varies according to the area that the agency protects, but much of it is simply hard, manual labor. The tools and equipment used by most forestry agencies are based on taking the fight directly to the seat of the fire. The work often involves long hours of cutting brush with hand tools.

## U.S. Fire Administration and National Fire Academy

The Federal Emergency Management Agency (FEMA) operates the U.S. Fire Administration (USFA) and the National Fire Academy (NFA). The USFA oversees the programs that deal with a wide range of fire protection subjects, such as firefighter safety, research on fire problems, and the development of materials to support the efforts of other fire fighting agencies. The NFA operates a training and education facility at Emmittsburg, Pennsylvania, for instructing fire officers in dealing with local and state fire problems.

## Miscellaneous Agencies

There are several other federal agencies with jobs related to fire protection, but the positions vary from time to time, depending upon budgetary decisions of the current federal administration. For example, fire protection jobs may be available in the State Department, the Department of Commerce, and the Consumer Products Safety Commission. The number of positions and the level of entry requirements vary considerably.

## Summary

Although the firefighter is the most visible fire service person, there are many other functions in a modern fire department. The spectrum of job opportunities is sufficiently diverse to offer something for anyone who aspires to enter the field. Interest and effort on the part of the individual are paramount. You can almost always locate one or more positions in the fire service, regardless of personal skills and physical capabilities. It takes a lot of work, but the rewards are great. There are few other occupations that offer not only a good public image but an exciting and challenging career as well.

# 3

---

# A Day in the Life of a
# Fire Department

THERE ARE SOME jobs in which you never have to worry about what your day is going to be like. Day in and day out, the work is the same. No surprises, no changes. But not so in the fire service! Every workday brings new challenges and new dimensions to the job.

When people choose the fire service as a career, they also accept that it is necessary to be involved in situations that may or may not be under their control. The work world of the firefighter is full of routine—yet full of danger. In any given day on the job, one can go from performing some mundane task like painting a fire hydrant to physically rescuing someone from a burning building in fewer than ten minutes. In some ways, this unpredictability is the attraction of the fire service; in other ways, it is a liability.

This chapter is limited to the fire combat role in order to provide a sense of perspective. In other chapters, we discuss several related jobs that have different types of workdays. In the interest of time and space, this section will deal only with the entry-level firefighter situation.

## Fire Department Organization

Typically firefighters are assigned to crews that are called *companies*. A fire company usually consists of an officer, an apparatus operator, and one or two firefighters. They are normally assigned and known by a specific piece of fire equipment, like an engine company or pumper company or sometimes an aerial ladder or truck company. Depending on local conditions, there may be one or two fire companies assigned to each fire station. Normally fire companies are assigned to work shifts. These shifts vary from department to department. In most of the country, the shifts are for a twenty-four-hour period. In some parts of the country, the shifts are for ten or fourteen hours and the crews periodically rotate from day to night shift.

Each shift is referred to as a *platoon*. Typically a platoon or shift is referenced by the letters A, B, or C. If a department has more than five or six fire stations, a platoon is broken down into *battalions*. These are groupings of fire companies that protect specific geographical areas and operate under the command of one chief officer. In large cities, there may even be many different battalions.

Another aspect of the life of the firefighter is the fact that the fire station is like a home away from home. Because they work in shifts and in companies, workers in the fire service tend to be very fraternal. When a person has to spend an entire twenty-four-hour shift with another person, a type of bonding occurs that is very different from that in other jobs. Firefighters must eat together, they must work together, and they must face danger together. There are very few jobs where camaraderie and the spirit of cooperation are as important as they are in the fire service.

To show how a work shift for a firefighter might involve several of these factors, we will follow an imaginary firefighter from the time the shift starts to the following morning when the shift goes off-duty. Granted, there are days when a firefighter can be bored to death, but they are in the minority. The majority of the shifts that a firefighter works will resemble the following scenario. The actual amount and intensity of the activity varies a great deal. Fire company workloads usually depend on the type of community served—industrial, urban, or isolated.

## Fictional Firefighter Mike Johnson at Work

Some people just show up for work. They don't concern them-selves about what has happened while they were gone, and they don't care what happens after they leave. Firefighter Mike Johnson doesn't feel that way, for a very good reason. He is assigned to the truck company, a one-hundred-foot aerial ladder company. What has happened since he left the station twenty-four hours before may affect his life in the next twenty-four hours. As he enters the fire station from the back of the dormitory, he notices that the hose tower is full of wet fire hose. Yesterday wasn't scheduled for a wet hose lay drill, so that could mean that the crew fought fire yesterday.

The observation is reinforced as he pours himself the first cup of coffee for the day. The A shift is up and about, but that's about all. Sprawled in the chairs around the room, they exhibit the famil-iar characteristics of people who have been up all night. They are groggy and anxious for some sleep. They are tired but retain their sense of humor. Mike notes that the two captains are in the office with the door closed. His captain will assume command of the shift at 0800 hours (8:00 A.M.). His captain is talking in an animated fashion with the other captain.

The contrast between the oncoming shift and the one going off is stark. Mike and the rest of B shift are in crisp, clean uniforms and look ready to assume their duties. The A shift, on the other hand, looks thrashed. Most are in their turnout clothing, with rumpled T-shirts rudely tucked into their pants and haggard faces showing the signs of stress and lack of sleep.

Tiredness doesn't affect the banter, however. Customarily shift changes in the firehouse serve three purposes. The first is to exchange important information about broken or missing equipment and to discuss new policies and procedures and work that cannot wait until the shift returns. The second purpose is to formally exchange responsibility from one shift to the other: one company logs out, the other logs in. The third reason is to catch up on the latest gossip, jokes, and rumors.

No one is exempt. The two shifts overlap for a period of about thirty minutes to carry out the ritual. During that interval, Mike discovers that the air cylinders in the breathing apparatus on Truck One need to be dealt with immediately. Last night's fire depleted the bottles below departmental standards. They need to be refilled, and that will be top priority. The entire crew's life may depend on that air sometime later that same day.

As soon as those in the off-going shift gather their personal belongings and leave, an air of calm comes over the station. For about ten minutes the crew merely sits around, sipping second cups of coffee and reading the material on the clipboard and bulletin boards. The captain turns on the computer and collects the

E-mail for the last twenty-four hours. Presently the company officer emerges from the office; he spends the remainder of the shift-exchange period going over the day's work schedule with the crew. As usual, the emphasis is on readiness and routine. The officer has a full schedule of events for the day.

Mike knows without direction that the top priority is to make sure that Truck One will be ready to answer the bell. Other activities for the day are prioritized, too, but all in descending order from the duty to be ready to roll. While the captain reviews the schedule, Mike makes mental notes on the details of his responsibilities in the completion of the day's tasks. Today the tasks range from the menial to the mentally demanding. The station kitchen is to be dutied, that is, given a special amount of attention during its cleaning, and there is a prefire planning session at the chemical plant.

## Daily Discipline

When the crew splits up, each member does her or his tasks with a minimum of supervision. The officer returns to the office to begin the paperwork for the day. Mike is assigned to the dormitory and rest room area. He goes to the apparatus room and helps the apparatus operator get the bottles back in shape on the breathing apparatus. The crew of the engine company busily checks the inventory of the engine.

Housekeeping is always a chore, but in a fire station it is an essential part of a disciplined lifestyle. Mike and firefighter Jan Evans from the truck company spend an hour getting the station into proper shape; they square away the beds and clean the rest room thoroughly. Inasmuch as fire stations employ several shifts of personnel, cleanliness is essential to good health and compatibility. The other shifts did their part by keeping the debris of the former night to a minimum. In the firehouse tradition, everyone picks up after herself or himself. Mike and his partner make sure that all facilities are ready for inspection.

The captain of the engine company calls his crew for coffee break a little earlier than the truck company. The engine company is due to go to the drill tower at 1000 hours (10:00 A.M.) for a series of drills on hose handling under supervision of the department's training officer. Sometimes Mike and the truck company train with the engine company, but today they work separately. While the personnel on the engine prepare for their drill, Mike helps the engineer of the truck company finish. Mike will be taking an examination for the job of apparatus operator in less than six months, so he never turns down a chance to operate the equipment.

With a belch of gray-blue diesel smoke, the engine company crew leaves the station and heads for the training tower. The two crews exchange comments about what "real" firefighters would be doing during their day. Mike feels a pang of remorse about not getting to engage in the physical task of pulling and stretching the fire hose. Today he will perform inspections. Although the task seems to pale in comparison, it is just as important as the more visible job of fire suppression.

## Fire Call

Just as they sit down at the dining room table, the first bell sounds. As the dispatcher calls out the address and response district, Mike moves quickly to his position on the truck company. The call is for a reported structure fire in an apartment complex. Putting on his turnout coat, Mike mentally reviews what he knows about the complex. Access, type of construction, shapes of buildings, and such other pieces of information come quickly to mind because he has been in the buildings many times on pre-plans or inspections.

The siren on the truck has just barely gone through its second oscillation when the engine company reports that they are on the scene and can handle the call. Conflicting feelings ripple through Mike's mind: a combination of relief that the fire is not serious and a sense of frustration caused by being geared up for the fight and then being brought back down so quickly. Once Mike had admitted these conflicting feelings to an old veteran firefighter, who had confessed to Mike that he had them, too, and would probably have them until the day he retired.

## Prefire Planning Session

The crew never finishes the coffee break. They are scheduled to be at the chemical plant at 1030 hours (10:30 A.M.). The captain does not want to be late, so they just gather the necessary paperwork. The captain has a sheaf of papers about the plant on the clipboard, including a plot plan of the structure, records of previous inspections, some inspection guidelines, and various reports to be submitted after the inspection.

As they drive to the plant, Mike reflects on the fact that since becoming a firefighter three years ago, he has been inside practically every commercial structure they pass. He has spent hundreds of hours learning the anatomy of the business and industrial communities. He knows thousands of details about the district that he responds to, and it never seems to stop. The more he learns the more he finds to learn.

The inspection doesn't take long. The captain meets with the plant manager. They take a brief tour around the exterior of the plant and then go into the buildings. The apparatus driver stays on the rig, in case a call comes in. One hour later the crew emerges. They have checked exits, looked at electrical panels, reviewed the inspection dates on fire protection systems, and discovered that a new ethylene oxide tank has been installed in the rear of one of the buildings. That information will have to be relayed to the fire marshal, to be put on the bureau's records.

## Mealtime at the Station

Lunch is uneventful, except that the rookie Tim Kelly prepares it. Tim is the newest member of Truck One. Although he is enthusiastic, his culinary skills are somewhat lacking. Typically, the task of preparing meals rotates among the members of the fire company. This usually ensures that one or more of the meals served during a shift will provide the energy necessary to survive those twenty-four hours. Tim underestimates the appetites of the eleven crew members assigned to headquarters and comes up a bit short of helpings.

Truck One and Engine One eat together most of the time. Mealtime in the fire station is an important part of the lifestyle of the firefighter. Firefighters always seem to be together on drills, on emergencies, and at the meal table. Much of the camaraderie on the team begins at the dining room table and is then tested on the foreground.

The first part of the afternoon is devoted to a little more housekeeping. After the meal is cleaned up, the crew goes about the task of straightening the station again. Mike turns on the television while the others read or talk about plans for their days off. They return to work at 1300 hours (1:00 p.m.).

## Public Assist Call

The bells sound for the second time during the shift at 1342 hours (1:42 P.M.). This time the call is for a public assist. A woman let her three-year-old granddaughter go into the bathroom by herself. The child played with the lock and locked herself in the bathroom. A Code Two response (no red lights and sirens) to the scene puts Mike and the crew at the scene within five minutes of the panicked call to the dispatch center. Eleven minutes later the frightened child and grateful grandmother are reunited.

## Daily Training

At 1520 hours (3:20 P.M.) the captain announces the drill for the day. The engine company has already done its training for the day, so it will not be a multicompany drill. About thirty minutes earlier, the engine company had left the station to perform in-service fire inspections of the business community. This week they were concentrating on public assemblies, like restaurants and theaters.

Today's training for the truck company relates to the activities of the engine company counterparts; the drill is on high-rise fire fighting tactics. A lot of the details that firefighters need to know to fight a high-rise fire are founded in good fire prevention practices.

Training is a type of prevention, too. Mike has never fought a high-rise fire. In fact, he has never even seen one, but he has the knowledge he needs to face the event when it happens. His training at the recruit academy and in his classes at the community college have prepared him to combat fire above the reaches of the aerial apparatus to which he is assigned. This is necessary in order to have enough personnel available to help the public to safety in a high-rise incident. All of his training is designed to prevent injury to himself or his fellow crew members.

The drill is supposed to end at 1700 hours (5:00 p.m.), but the clanging of the station bells ends it prematurely. The dispatcher received several calls simultaneously. The first is from a citizen on the emergency telephone line. The second is from the police department dispatcher. Skillfully, the fire department dispatcher handles the telephones and the radios to get the information to the fire companies.

## Traffic Rescue

This time the call is for a traffic collision—cut and rescue. Response to the scene is Code Three (red light and siren). Donning their heavy turnout coats, pants, boots, and helmets, crew members take their positions on the truck.

Mike shares the concern of the others on the rig as they roll through intersection after intersection. This type of alarm calls for multiple companies to respond. That always creates danger to the companies because sometimes they cannot hear each other as they come to the intersections. Arriving at the scene of the collision, Mike sees that all the other units are already there. The paramedics are inside the badly twisted wreck, administering medical aid to the trapped victim.

In a matter of moments, the truck crew unloads the hydraulic rescue tool, the air chisel, and the come-alongs. Working in close coordination with the other crews, the captain stabilizes the vehicle so that it will not roll any more and endanger the crews. While the engine company lays hose lines to fight any potential fire in the spilled fuel, Mike puts on goggles and heavy gloves. Performing like a well-rehearsed dance team, the crew members work to remove the trapped victim. Mike operates the Jaws of Life. This powerful hydraulic tool tears at the sheet metal that holds the victim in the vehicle. Another crew member cuts the seat belt and then the seat bolts, so that the victim can be moved. The come-alongs (which are like block-and-tackle devices) are used to pull the steering wheel up and out of the way.

The sound of the pulsating hydraulic tool and the hammering air chisel are normal sounds to the crew. The paramedics work closely with the victim and warn him what to expect. Each of the paramedics has to be carefully garbed in rubber gloves and other protection to prevent contact with body fluids. Communicable diseases can affect emergency responses quickly under these conditions, so extra effort is taken to prevent contact with these contaminants—called blood-borne pathogens. Each move is calculated to do the least possible amount of damage to the trapped person. Nothing is done without being coordinated among all crew members.

The paramedics working on the trapped victim maintain radio contact with the emergency room at the local hospital. After diagnosing the person's injuries, they transmit that information to a doctor. After only a few moments' consultation, they receive orders to administer an intravenous solution and give the victim some drugs to counter the effects of the injury.

To the onlooker, the crews appear to be moving slowly. Several civilians standing behind the police lines offer advice and criticism about the way that the operation is going. Mike knows, however, that speed is secondary to accuracy. A slip of those powerful hydraulic tools can cripple a person for life.

The crew uses its time carefully, and shortly the victim is in the ambulance and on the way to the hospital. The return to the station, without benefit of red light and siren, takes more than twice as long as the original response. Dinner is not served until almost 1930 hours (7:30 p.m.).

## A Quiet Evening

After 2000 hours (8:00 p.m.), the crew relaxes and hopes that the rest of the shift will remain quiet. The chances of that are slim, for it is a matter of record that most of the deadly fires occur during the wee hours of the morning. Things like cooking, heating, and hobby activities lead to circumstances requiring assistance from the fire department. More emergencies occur between 7:00 p.m. and 7:00 a.m. than vice versa.

The only interruption of the evening's activities is a few telephone calls from the outlying stations. The battalion chief, who is responsible for the entire on-duty shift, stays at the station during the evening hours, so there tend to be more telephone calls than usual. Mike spends the evening studying a hydraulics textbook. Because of the number of candidates for the next exam, he knows that he must understand the material well. He, like most of the others, goes to bed at around 2130 hours (9:30 p.m.).

## Late-Night Fire Call

He doesn't stay in bed for long. The dispatcher's voice over the loudspeaker and the activation of the bells awaken Mike instantly. The announcement is for a reported structure fire in Engine Three's first-in area, the area for which it has primary responsibility. Engine One and Truck One are due to act as backup. Engine Three does not have a truck company in quarters, so Truck One is the first-due truck. Quickly rolling out of bed, the entire crew gets into their turnout clothing, snapping suspenders into place as they tromp out of the dorm onto the apparatus-room floor. The lights have been turned on by the relays that activated the alarms.

Engine One rolls first. The truck emerges into the cold night air, squealing its tires as it makes the first intersection. The siren is briefly overpowered by the sound of the air horn. Mike knows from the address that the response is to a three-story courtyard apartment complex. As the apparatus driver steers the one-hundred-foot aerial through the somewhat abandoned streets, Mike reviews the checklist of possible tasks he may need to perform in the first few minutes on the scene—ventilation, rescue, forcible entry, salvage. A combination of training and anticipation gained from going to so many near misses has given him a sense of fate: this is going to be a worker.

As the truck follows the engine through the streets, the firefighters see the column of smoke billowing over the tops of the other structures. Even at night, smoke is visible. The lights of the city reflect off the convoluted and animated edges of the brown-gray smoke cloud. Getting closer, the truck crew sees that the smoke comes from the top apartment of the three-story building. Engine Three issues orders by radio to each arriving company.

Mike doesn't worry about these orders. The captain worries about them instead, and Mike listens to orders from his officer. He never second-guesses the captain. Some of his actions are automatic, as part of standard operating procedures. Disembarking from the aerial, he immediately puts on steel tanks to carry his breathing air. The captain orders two men to the interior, to help the engine crew ventilate the building. Both he and Mike know, however, that the fire is in the attic and spreading to the other apartments.

The officer orders the apparatus operator to "ladder the building." Moving quickly to the apparatus jacks, Mike assists in lowering the massive legs to the ground to stabilize the tall aerial ladder. Each member of the crew performs as if programmed. Moving to the turntable, the engineer raises the ladder from its bed and begins raising, rotating, and extending the ladder. Ultimately, the ladder rests on the roof's edge.

Mike grabs an ax; the captain has a pike pole (a short pole with a hook on it). The remaining truck crew member grabs another ax. Together, the three of them, looking like a cross between ancient gladiators and modern astronauts, climb the ladder to the edge of the roof. The captain also conducts periodic conversations on a pack-set radio. The captain must coordinate the work with the firefighters operating the nozzles below. The three dismount the ladder and move to the peak of the roof, directly over the apartment where the fire seems to be. Mike moves cautiously on the roof, checking for softness of the roof from time to time.

It does not pay to be careless in a firefight. Many firefighters have fallen through a roof into an inferno because they failed to check their path. Mike is young and inexperienced, but well trained. Taking the precaution seems natural. After finding the spot, the crew cuts a hole six feet square in the roof so that hot air from the building has a place to escape. This may sound easy, but it isn't when you are wearing forty-five to fifty-five pounds of equipment on your back and getting all of your breathing air through a little tube fed by the steel tank on your back. The job takes fewer than six minutes, but it seems like sixty.

As soon as the hole is finished, the truck company returns to the ground. The job is not over. The engine companies have been able to enter the building, but the area is far from secure. Engine crews are still lying on their bellies in the hot water that was coming off the walls and ceiling as the fire was extinguished. The truck crew continues going in, to cross-ventilate the rest of the area. Huge fans called smoke ejectors hang in the windows to blow out the smoke and products of combustion created by the fire's spread.

The apartments below the burning apartment are now subject to damage from the water running off the fire. The truck company's job is to get salvage covers over personal property as quickly as possible. The captain regroups the crew as soon as the fire is declared under control. Mike and one other crew member are assigned to set up lights for the interior of the building. Earlier one of the engine companies had cut off the utilities to the building as a safety precaution, so they now have no lights.

Although the actual firefight only takes about twenty-five minutes, the work has just begun. There is fire in the walls of the building, requiring a lot of overhaul. Meanwhile the engine personnel roll up the large hose lines. Truck personnel continue extending electrical cords to take lights into every nook and cranny. Upon finishing that task, Mike uses the infrared heat scanner to check the burned areas around windows and doors.

After one hour and forty-five minutes, the truck company is released. The engine company leaves sooner, because they have hose and equipment to repack. Rolling back to the station, Mike notices that no matter how cold it is in the morning when you leave to go to the fire, it always seems colder when you are returning to the station. Scrunching down in the jump seat, the young firefighter remembers that his wet turnouts make it seem much colder on the tailboard of the truck.

### *Back to the Station*

The clock registers 0342 hours (3:42 A.M.) when the cold turnouts are shed and the covers turned back on the bed. Mike falls into a fitful sleep. His sleep is disturbed one more time, at 0515 hours (5:15 A.M.) when Engine One is called out to respond to a medical aid. The engine and the paramedics handle it. When they return to the station, they make coffee and get ready to greet the oncoming C shift. Mike gives up on sleep at 0615 hours (6:15 A.M.) and joins the rest of the crew in the coffee room.

At 0800 hours (8:00 A.M.), the ritual of shift exchange occurs again. Eleven fresh, uniformed firefighters come to the station; eleven rumpled, tired bodies prepare to leave the station. Mike goes to his locker, changes into a sweat suit, and prepares to ride his bicycle to his apartment.

This had not been his first shift, so he wasn't that excited. This had not been his last shift, so he wasn't bored. He has a lot more of this to look forward to. He knows, as he closes the door behind him, that every shift he works will be a kaleidoscope of events and activities. Over his career he will deal with death and destruction, but also with life and the preservation of property.

All in all, it was a good day's work!

## Summary

There you have it—a typical day in the life of a fire company. The scenarios can vary considerably. It's not uncommon for a firefighter to respond to an average of about five emergencies during any given shift. Some crews, like airport crash crews or fireboats, get only one or two calls a week. Other crews, such as those in the inner cities, run every hour on the hour. From the largest to the smallest of fire departments, the responsibility never changes, only the frequency with which their members are called upon to test themselves under emergency conditions.

Some of the topics that firefighters are training on are changing. For example, many fire agencies are now involved in learning more about weapons of mass destruction as a result of terrorist activities. Others are learning more about communicable diseases and ways of dealing with epidemics. The way that firefighters are learning is changing too. Television, once a source of entertainment, is now being used to bring comprehensive training topics right into the fire station over satellite or cable. Long-distance learning modules are being made available that will allow firefighters to obtain much-needed training and even certification over the Internet.

The one main point to remember about the job of a firefighter is that it is a dangerous and demanding occupation. It requires a unique combination of mental alertness and physical capability to perform the job safely.

# 4

---

# PRIVATE FIRE PROTECTION CAREERS

MOST INDIVIDUALS INTERESTED in getting into the fire profession start by pursuing one or more of the jobs discussed in previous chapters. A person may fail to achieve a job in public fire protection—or prefer to pursue opportunities in private fire protection—for a variety of reasons, including the following:

- **Competition.** For every job in the fire fighting profession, there may be hundreds of candidates. This may force an interested person to seek an alternative fire protection career.
- **Stringent physical demands.** There are thousands of candidates who are equal to the mental challenge of fire protection but who cannot meet the physical demands of strength and agility. Very small physical flaws, such as a

minor spinal defect or color blindness, can cause a person to be eliminated from consideration.

- **The intellectual challenge of private enterprise fire protection engineering.** Very few fire fighting agencies employ fire protection engineers, but almost all of the major industries do. This aspect of fire protection is often more challenging and financially rewarding than municipal fire protection.
- **The future.** Over the past few decades, more and more emphasis has been placed on private fire protection. It is anticipated that this trend will continue well into the future.

One should not consider private fire protection to be second best. Private fire protection contains some of the greatest challenges in the profession. The only difference is in public perception, in which public fire departments are viewed as the primary fire protection. Many of the jobs we will discuss in this chapter require a great deal of education and experience.

There are probably more people involved in fire protection in the private sector than in the public sector. The jobs are not obvious, however, and most of them do not deal with emergencies. They focus on either prevention or preparation for emergencies.

## Private Fire Departments

Private fire departments are not financed or managed by any level of the government. Most of them are in the petrochemical, aircraft, or aerospace industries. These fire departments protect very specific facilities. A classic example of such a private fire department can be seen at companies such as Boeing and McDonnell Douglas. Some very large security firms like Wackenhut also provide private fire protection services as a part of a total security system for airports or chemical plants.

Probably one of the most famous firefighters in the world is the private firefighter Red Adair. A film starring John Wayne was once made about his life and the tremendous challenges he faced while fighting oil fires. But, one does not become a freelance firefighter. Private fire departments are structured much like public ones. The point of entry is at the rookie level, the departments are paramilitary in nature, and the actual jobs performed are very similar.

The biggest distinction is that private fire departments usually serve only one very specific area and are highly specialized. Some private fire departments protect facilities that cost millions of dollars more than the surrounding communities served by the municipal fire departments. Often these jobs require a great deal of time on fire inspection to make sure that all precautions are taken to prevent a catastrophe from occurring.

There are many providers of private fire protection services in the United States. The largest of these is the Rural-Metro Corporation in Scottsdale, Arizona. Although no records have been published regarding the number of communities that have private fire departments, it is known that there are private departments in Alaska, Arizona, Georgia, Illinois, and Oregon.

## Fire Alarm Companies

The fire alarm industry is closely related to the burglar alarm industry, but is definitely a part of the fire protection field. Fire alarm companies install, maintain, and repair such things as smoke detectors, heat alarms, and automatic notification devices. They work in the field of electronics and mechanical equipment. It is not uncommon for fire alarm companies to maintain computers and extensive digital communications equipment.

People who work in this field have to be qualified to work on sophisticated equipment. They may also need experience in building construction. Because fire alarm companies have such free access to property, their employees must be trustworthy and bonded (insured against improper acts while on duty).

## Fire Extinguisher Companies

Many members of the fire service got their first jobs in the field of fire extinguisher maintenance. Almost every community has a need for a company to distribute, maintain, and repair fire extinguishers and fixed fire-protection equipment. This job is somewhat technical in nature and requires that an individual carefully follow instructions and comply with laws and regulations.

In most states, fire extinguisher maintenance people are licensed or certified to perform their function. You can imagine what would happen if someone needed to use a fire extinguisher that had not been properly maintained. This job has a lot of responsibility and carries with it a degree of liability.

## Fire Sprinkler Companies

Related to the fire extinguisher field, but more complex, is the field of automatic fire protection equipment. Most communities now require automatic fire sprinklers in high-rise buildings and industrial structures. There is also a very large industry that involves installing fire extinguisher systems in hoods and ducts in restaurants. Some companies specialize in installing built-in fire equipment for such facilities as aircraft hangars or warehouses.

On the surface, these jobs no more resemble a conventional fire department than the Wright Brothers' aircraft looks like a DC-10. But don't be misled. Modern fire protection increasingly depends on the installation and use of built-in fire protection. Most people do not want to spend an entire lifetime filling fire extinguishers or installing automatic sprinkler systems. However, in an entry-level job in one of these related occupations, one may gather valuable experience toward becoming competitive for the jobs in fire departments.

Most entry-level jobs in this area of fire protection are mechanical. They are also very technical in nature. They require an ability to use one's hands in conjunction with following somewhat complicated diagrams and plans. The work is often dirty and the hours long. Depending on the particular craft involved, the pay varies from low to very high. Promotions and the variety of work are often limited, unless the firm has a broad array of clients.

## Fire Equipment Manufacturing or Sales

One of the most financially rewarding fields related to fire protection is the sales field. Many companies, such as Akron Brass and Darley Pumps, maintain sales staff to service the needs of fire departments. In this field, a person is assigned a certain area of the country in which to sell everything from fire trucks to fire hose. Most sales positions are given to people who are experienced in the field. Many of them are retired from the professional fire service.

On the other hand, many people who have not necessarily been in-service fire personnel but who have a working knowledge of the fire service are on the staffs of small fire equipment companies. This is especially true in the field of manufacturing. Companies that make fire equipment often hire skilled labor to produce the various pieces of fire equipment. In this respect, the hiring needs are very similar to those in the sprinkler industry, where the emphasis is on technical competency.

## Insurance Rating Offices

In many states, the insurance industries maintain staffs to work strictly on fire-related problems. Most of the companies that have gone in this direction utilize only individuals who have fire experience or education. Jobs in these rating bureaus (as in many arson investigations) usually go to retired professionals from the fire service or to registered fire protection engineers.

Fire insurance firms also have jobs in the fields of plan checking or arson investigation. Many of the larger companies have staffs to perform these highly technical tasks. Experienced fire officers fill most of these positions. Graduates from recognized fire protection schools fill others.

Although there are few entry-level jobs in the insurance industry, it still deserves a few moments of consideration. The continued emphasis on fire prevention and the transfer of fire protection to the private sector may create a resurgence of jobs in this area for those with the proper education.

## Fire Protection Engineers

If there is an unsung element of the fire service, it is the fire protection engineers. These are people who fight fire with codes and ordinances instead of nozzles and ladders. Fire protection engineering is a discipline, a field of specialization of engineering. It focuses on building into structures and installations the proper design so that fire will not occur or at least its effects will be minimized.

This job involves a great deal of planning and research. It also involves a great deal of paperwork and compliance with complex rules and regulations. Much of the design work also demands use of special tools like computers, calculators, and drafting equipment. Most of the work is mentally demanding, but it sometimes involves physical requirements as well. For example, a fire protection engineer may have to inspect the installations he or she has designed.

Depending upon the nature of the firm that employs a fire protection engineer, the work can be limited or diverse. Some of the types of firms that use fire protection engineers are architectural firms, large hotel and motel chains, automatic fire protection companies, chemical companies, aerospace organizations, and testing laboratories. Some people in this area of fire protection travel worldwide in the pursuit of their projects.

The educational curriculum of fire protection engineers is one of the most demanding. Few schools offer the discipline of fire protection engineering, and the competition is very keen. Because the curriculum involves some difficult subjects like chemistry and physics, it is not the type of education that one enters unless one has thoroughly explored the goal of the program.

Graduates of fire protection engineering programs never have to wait too long for jobs. With the continued emphasis on built-in fire protection and the increased complexity of fire codes, the fire protection engineer seems assured of a strong job market. Many progressive fire departments are now beginning to employ graduates of these programs in their fire prevention bureaus before they enter private practice. Fire protection engineers are also employed by the insurance industry, the automatic sprinkler industry, state fire marshals' offices, building departments, federal fire agencies, the military, and educational institutions.

As modern technology develops at an unprecedented rate, the fire protection engineer has an almost unlimited potential in the future. The varieties of problems that need such engineering expertise are inexhaustible.

## Summary

Although the public sector is where most of the entry-level fire protection jobs currently are, the private sector may well be a growing future job market. A combination of individual needs, the increased costs of government, and taxpayers' rejection of higher taxes may well force the issue. A person looking into fire protection careers should always keep his or her options open to apply for private sector positions.

# 5

## QUALIFICATIONS AND PERSONAL ASSESSMENT

ASPIRING TO A position in the fire service and actually being qualified for the job are two different things. Each year many people start to pursue a fire service career. Some are doomed to failure from the start; they do not know that there are definite qualifications for each fire service position. Without examining those qualifications, a person can take a lot of dead-end roads while competing for the various jobs. In this chapter, we will discuss a few of the basic qualifications to pursue this occupation. As a candidate for a fire service career, you should take care to assess your ability to meet these qualifications.

Today, as never before in the history of the fire service, the people who recruit and select fire service personnel are challenged by the need to be fair to each candidate. This challenge is made even greater by the responsibility to recruit and select only the best-qualified people to protect the interests of the public and to achieve diversity. The job of recruiting and selecting more efficient and effective candidates requires an in-depth understanding of what kind of person the fire service is looking for.

Fire service agencies often employ people in both combat and noncombat roles. There are distinct differences between the traits, skills, and abilities that are required to be a successful candidate in the two different realms. On the other hand, there are very strong similarities in the motivation of people who select fire service careers—the primary motivation being a strong desire to serve people. The modern fire service needs people in both areas to fulfill the mission of saving lives and property.

## Duties

The examples of duties for an entry-level firefighter might read as follows:

- Responds to fire and medical emergencies and follows instructions of superior officers or standard operating procedures in the laying of hose lines and raising of ladders, performing acts of rescue or ventilation, extinguishing fire, or participating in clean-up operations
- Cleans, maintains, and inspects equipment and fire stations
- Participates in training sessions and drills
- Participates in the inspection of buildings for purposes of enforcing fire regulations
- Performs routine investigation of emergencies to determine the cause

- Handles radio and telephone communications
- Drives rescue and ambulance vehicles when required
- Performs such other duties as may be required to protect life and property

Sounds like a tall order, doesn't it? That's what is expected of a firefighter in most fire agencies today. The extent of many of the duties varies according to the nature of the community, but they are basically the same everywhere.

As you read those tasks, you probably thought, "I don't know how to do those things." That's okay. The examples of duties in a job description are describing what a person will have to do after being selected, trained, and assigned. They represent things a person will have to learn how to do, not the things that he or she already knows how to do.

Note the emphasis on the physical aspects of the job. This will be used in setting up certain aspects of the testing process. The physical agility and the medical examination are based on this requirement. A person cannot be graded on how to pull hose, but it is valid to see if he or she has the strength to pick up several sections of the hose and carry it for a short distance.

## Desirable Qualifications

A typical entry-level firefighter's desirable qualifications announcement might look like this:

- Ability to learn the theory and principles of modern fire protection

- Ability to apply knowledge gained in training to practical operations under both routine and emergency conditions
- Ability to read and understand written instructions and training materials, maps, diagrams, and schematics for content and meaningfulness to assigned tasks
- Ability to adopt quick, reasonable, and effective courses of action under emergency conditions
- Ability to establish and maintain effective relationships with others

These criteria will be used in setting up the written examination and possibly an oral examination, so it is in a candidate's interest to pay attention to them.

## What About You Personally?

You've already decided to look into the fire service as a career or you wouldn't be so far along in this book. The big question is, "Should you be in the fire service?" What kind of a person makes a good candidate for this occupation? How can you assess your chances of employment before you waste a lot of time filling out applications and visiting fire agencies? According to a study done by the Minneapolis Civil Service Commission, "Firefighters who [do] better on the job [are] likely to be organized, dependable, hard-working, cautious and follow the directions of others." That may sound a little dull, but it is accurate.

The fire profession is highly reliant upon teamwork and dependability. People who have developed skills in these areas will fit in well. Desire to enter the service is not enough. You must develop a competitive edge.

# Basics

Among the most basic of knowledge, skills, and abilities is the need to know your physical limitations. Many of the functions of the firefighter require peak physical demands. Strength alone is not enough. Agility and endurance are needed as well. The physical aspects are less important in staff jobs and as a person is promoted to higher ranks in the fire service, but physical skills are paramount at the entry level in suppression jobs.

## *Physical Fitness*

One of the best ways to prepare yourself in this area is to engage in organized sports activities. Generally, those sports that require combinations of speed, strength, endurance, and teamwork are the best training grounds. Sports like baseball, basketball, soccer, football, and hockey are excellent for developing motor skills and coordination.

As you may recall from the Minneapolis study, firefighters need to be capable of accepting directions easily. That comes from team sports also. A fire company is very much like a small sports team. Most firefighters continue to participate in sports in their spare time, and many fire departments have sports teams or engage in sports activities as part of a physical fitness program.

As a potential candidate, you are well advised to do everything you can to get in shape and stay in shape. Sometimes a person cannot engage in team sports because of family responsibilities, but one can almost always develop some sort of physical fitness program. It is far better to start the process as early as possible than to try to get in shape quickly for a competitive test.

An entry-level test in the physical area may include such things as picking up fire hose and carrying or dragging it for a distance. That may not sound like much, but fire hose can weigh a lot when it includes brass couplings, many gallons of water, and several connected sections. The test may include such tasks as removing a large ladder from the side of an existing piece of fire apparatus or picking up a large fan—called a smoke ejector—and hanging it from a window. Sometimes tests include raising the fly (a section of a ladder) on a large extension ladder. All of these tests require specific levels of strength.

Other types of physical tests may include having candidates climb a high ladder to determine if they have acrophobia (fear of heights). Some departments also test candidates for claustrophobia (fear of confinement). This test consists of putting a candidate into a breathing apparatus and blacking out the masks. Then the candidate is asked to perform some physical task. If the fear of confinement is there, it quickly becomes evident.

## Academic Competence

Someone once said that to be a good firefighter, you have to know a little bit about the basics of almost twenty-three different occupations. Firefighters deal in construction, chemistry, electronics, mathematics, law, and medicine almost every day. Basic knowledge of reading, writing, and arithmetic is essential.

That may seem obvious, but it isn't. Many potential candidates are excluded in the competitive process because they lack these skills. Literacy is just as important to the modern firefighter as are physical skills. As the fire service moves toward more automation and sophistication in practices and procedures, it will become even more important.

We are not talking about exceptional intelligence. Fire fighting does not require a high IQ, but it does require normal intelligence and some basic academic skills.

If you are now a high school or college student, it may be difficult to see how a class in English composition is going to relate to the job of a firefighter. But there is a correlation. The first time you have to complete a report for an officer or appear in court to testify about an incident report, you will discover the value of good writing. And when a firefighter is sent to an overturned tanker on the interstate at three o'clock in the morning, it helps to know the difference between the behaviors of liquid and gas. That knowledge may make the difference between a good decision and a dangerous one.

Fire agencies teach their employees these subjects, but that instruction is not an adequate substitute for formal education. Furthermore, if you cannot learn the basic subjects in school, you may not be able to learn them in the fire service either. The fire service must hire people who can learn quickly.

Master those basics. Don't be fooled by the physical aspects of fire protection. It is a thinking person's profession, too. Competition for these jobs is keen. Don't overlook the value of developing competitive skills while still in school. Getting a grade of *C* might get you through algebra in your school, but it won't get you the job if someone else has an *A* and can beat you out on the test. The jobs will go to the people who best demonstrate the required skills.

Many people are lulled into complacency in this area because many agencies have dropped high school education as a requirement to take an entry-level test. Departments have dropped that requirement in some cases to eliminate discrimination against people who have the skill but lack the diploma. But be careful. The test criteria are still job-related. It is possible to complete high school and never develop the right skills. It is also possible to drop out of high school and still develop one's skills to a high level.

Don't just get a high school or college diploma, get a high school or college education. Maximize your participation in subject areas to give yourself that competitive edge in written examinations.

## Background

You should also consider what you could do for yourself in the area of personal background. Some of these things do not sound too significant, but they can be important factors in test competition. A person should strive to maintain good driving, credit, and work records while awaiting the opportunity to test for fire service jobs.

Your driving record isn't really a problem in terms of competition unless it has moving violations on it. Fire personnel are expected to drive a variety of government vehicles. A person with a bad driving record is a poor risk for a department; a serious driving record can result in a candidate being removed from eligibility.

Any type of criminal record is also a liability, especially if it involves theft or narcotics. These can be a real problem because firefighters live in such close quarters that they are vulnerable to theft; lockers are left open when an emergency call comes in, and watches and wallets are often in plain view. Firefighters must be able to trust their coworkers, whether with their possessions or their lives. Narcotics problems are a real conflict because many fire agencies must carry controlled substances as part of their paramedic programs. These drugs are closely controlled, but they are still part of the station environment. Obviously, a firefighter tempted to use drugs is not a reliable member of the team. Departments are very leery of candidates who have any criminal record.

Credit records and good job references are helpful, too. Although none of these areas are examined during the testing period, they are often considered before actual selection begins. Remember the quote from the Minneapolis study that referred to the fact that firefighters tend to be dependable people? The credit and work record is one of the first places in which this behavioral characteristic demonstrates itself.

A person should cultivate a good list of references—not only friends, but respected people in the community who can verify a person's character. Classic examples of good references are teachers, counselors, clergy, businesspeople, and local government officials. You can acquire a lot of friends and still not have any good references. Most applications today do not ask for references; they are seldom used to exclude a person. But that doesn't mean we need to disregard them. It merely means that we should aspire to them for a different purpose.

By developing a good work record, you will develop job skills. That will help you in the competition. By cultivating good references, you will develop people skills and acquire mentors who will help you compete. A mentor is like a coach or counselor. Many times the people you obtain as references will share with you the insight they have used to become successful themselves. If you obtain a mentor who has fire service experience, that can be invaluable.

## Personal Traits

We have discussed the potential for physical fitness and academic preparation, but your personal characteristics enter into the process, too. You may think that you are a pretty good person; you may be well liked and even a popular person. Does that qualify you for the fire service? It's a good start, but let's look at some traits that have come from firefighter selection studies.

All of the following traits have been identified as characteristic of fire service candidates. As you review the list, think about each item and ask yourself, "How well do I meet that criterion?"

- Thinks and acts quickly
- Learns quickly
- Adapts to routine duties
- Exercises sound judgment
- Demonstrates initiative
- Acts unselfishly
- Exhibits calm under stress
- Demonstrates mechanical aptitude
- Demonstrates resourcefulness and ability to improvise
- Demonstrates ability to follow orders and procedures
- Is self-disciplined
- Demonstrates good work habits
- Adapts to working under adverse conditions
- Gets along with others in a group
- Has a sense of personal responsibility

# Summary

Not everyone wants to enter the fire service. Not everyone who wants to will be successful. We have discussed a few of the characteristics you should consider and steps you can take to increase your chances of getting into the service. Preparation is an important part of building professionalism. We have explored some of the basic qualifications in this text, but some of the criteria will be upgraded in the near future.

Those reading this text should be more sensitive to the act of preparation and, therefore, be ready for possible changes in criteria. Probably the best example of this possibility is the fact that many fire departments are now requiring some levels of pre-entry training for candidates. Some departments even have pre-entry certification requirements. As these concepts gain in momentum, they raise the level of achievement of each generation of the fire service. This raises the professional level of the occupation and makes it even more important for the candidate to be prepared.

# 6

## SALARIES AND BENEFITS

THERE ARE A couple of things you will never have to worry about if you decide to enter the fire service. The first is that you will probably never become a millionaire, but the second is that you will probably never have to worry about losing your job. The fire service is not among the highest paying of occupations, but the salaries are well within the range of being livable. The occupation's primary benefit is that it is among the most stable of jobs.

In many occupations, salary and security are inversely proportionate with one another. Jobs that pay very well can sometimes be filled with insecurity, and some jobs that are very stable may not pay well at all. The fire service combines the best of the two worlds. It pays fairly well and is relatively free of fluctuations in employment conditions.

## Advantages and Disadvantages

Like any other occupation, the fire service has its advantages and its disadvantages, some of which can be measured in dollars and cents. Most, however, cannot. The greatest asset of a fire service career cannot ever be given a monetary value: it is the sense of usefulness that a person feels by being a firefighter. Nothing can exceed the fulfillment a person gets by saving a life or winning a battle against a fire. It's an internal thing that does not show up on the paycheck, but most members of the fire service feel it and believe it.

Members of the fire service enjoy a camaraderie and fraternity that stretches across the nation. A firefighter from New York can feel very comfortable in the training room of a fire station in southern California. Firefighters often have as their hobby the collecting of fire memorabilia. They often hold giant musters, or contests, to test their skills. The greatest asset of the fire service is that it is never just a job, it is a lifetime commitment.

On the negative side of the ledger, the greatest liability of the fire service is that it is one of the most dangerous jobs in the country. More than one hundred firefighters a year are killed in the line of duty. More people are killed or injured in the line of duty as firefighters than almost any other occupation. Although this is certainly nothing to brag about, it is a reality. The scene of an emergency is full of danger. The same things that have caused an emergency to exist in the first place often endanger the firefighter. In addition, being required to go from a sound sleep to a full response in seconds takes its toll on the heart and lungs.

Continued emphasis on safety over the past few decades has improved conditions somewhat. But fire situations are getting continually worse. The use of more hazardous materials creates more dangerous fires. The presence of many communicable diseases that can be transferred by body fluids create a danger for those who are involved in emergency medical response. The incidence of more high-rise fires creates greater stress on fire crews. For these reasons, firefighters often have much better retirement systems than do other employees. They also have higher worker's compensation and disability claims, but many firefighters never reach retirement age.

Overall, however, the fire service is well compensated for the duties that it is expected to perform. The following are descriptions of the basic salary and benefits that a person can expect from a fire service career.

## Salaries

There are at least three different benchmarks that relate to the subject of salary: starting pay, range of pay, and highest pay. This means that a candidate needs to look carefully at salary schedules when competing for jobs. In any given area, these salary figures will vary a great deal, depending on such things as the size of the department and the community's ability to pay. You can actually find situations where two departments can be right next door to one another and have salaries that differ by as much as 20 percent.

According to the 2001 International City Managers Association (ICMA) Base-Line report, the average entry-level salary for full-time firefighters is about $29,350. This figure is an average of all areas of the country. Generally speaking, the high salaries are found in the largest cities, and the cities in the western part of the United States tend to be the highest. The lowest salaries tend to be in the departments that have part-time firefighters, especially through the Midwest.

The same report indicates that the average maximum salary for full-time firefighters is about $40,000. This is an increase of about 40 percent over the entry-level salary. Most of the cities that reported these data indicated that their salary schedules offered increases that would raise pay from the minimum to the maximum salary over a five-year period. This 4 to 5 percent annual increase is usually granted on the basis of improved performance on the job.

The Department of Labor updates the salary figures on a frequent basis for firefighters. It can be reviewed on the DOL website (bls.gov). According to the latest edition of the *Occupational Outlook Handbook* on that site, there were about 285,000 firefighter jobs on a full-time basis in 2002. This report states that firefighters can continue to expect keen competition for these jobs and that the number of firefighter jobs will likely increase more slowly than other occupations over the next ten years. However, it is also true that many fire agencies are seeing a major exodus of experienced people due to changes in the retirement systems and the normal retirement cycle that resulted from the employment boom of the 1970s and 1980s.

Some departments also offer what is called longevity pay. This is an extra, added salary (over the maximum salary) that is given to individuals who are very competent but who for some reason cannot or do not get promoted beyond the classification of firefighter. Longevity pay is not normally granted until the person has been on the job for an extended period of time. On the average, longevity pay increases maximum salaries by almost 6 percent. To be eligible for longevity pay, firefighters usually must have at least ten years of experience. The average for these longevity programs is around $1,000 per year added to the maximum salary.

Many fire agencies also give bonuses for different levels of educational achievement. These programs usually give a fixed amount for completing an associate of arts, a bachelor's degree, or even a master's degree in the field of fire protection.

A person who stays in the fire service until retirement can expect to be promoted at least once or twice within the hierarchy of the department. This will result in increasing salary levels. It is not uncommon for a person to reach a salary level of $80,000 per year as a chief officer.

## Unions in the Fire Service

One reason that the fire service has achieved many of its financial rewards is because of firefighter unions. Most of the larger departments are members of the International Association of Firefighters (IAFF). They are organized into groups called *locals*. Basically, a local is nothing more than a recognized group of firefighters from one department that has applied for recognition from the IAFF. The IAFF maintains a national office and works to protect the benefits of all firefighters. It sponsors legislation at the state and federal levels to increase these benefits whenever possible.

In most fire departments, union membership is not a requirement, nor does a person have to join the union to be considered for employment. In most cases, people cannot join until they have finished their probation. The dues to belong to the IAFF are usually nominal. IAFF officers are elected from among the ranks of the members by the members.

# Benefits

Of course, salary is only part of the compensation package that a firefighter receives. As a matter of fact, the benefits normally accrued to firefighters often equal as much as 50 percent of their base pay. Quite frankly, this is both a blessing and a curse for the fire service. It is good in that it provides a lot of protection for the members of the department. But it is a problem in that each year as budgets increase, the benefits paid to public safety personnel like those in fire and police departments are subject to criticism. The reason we mention it here is to warn potential firefighters that benefits must be used correctly and reserved for conditions where they are really needed. They should never be abused.

Among the benefits that we will discuss are retirement, disability, insurance, physical conditioning, allowances, educational incentives, sick leave and vacation, and intangible benefits.

## *Retirement*

Fire fighting is arduous and dangerous work. Because of the physical demands of the job, one cannot function as an entry-level firefighter or even a specialist or a combat officer much beyond the age of sixty. This does not mean that there aren't firefighters older than that. It means that, on the average, by the time a person has reached that age, he or she is no longer in the proper physical condition to be effective in emergencies.

For that reason, most fire agencies have retirement plans that release people from fire fighting duty before they reach a given age. These retirement plans are generally funded from two sources—the city and the individual. What generally occurs is that the local government agency will invest an amount of money equal to a percentage of a person's salary each month. The employee is asked to contribute a like amount. Over a period of years, this accumulates in a fund that will allow the person to retire at a certain age. The retirement amount frequently is equal to about 2 percent a year of a person's salary.

What this means is that people with twenty-five years on the job can retire with an income equal to about 50 percent of their base salary. This figure depends on the formula used by the employer and varies a great deal from one area to another. Also, this type of formula is usually used only for the uniformed members of the force. Nonuniformed members usually have a separate system.

## Disability

Fire fighting is among the most dangerous jobs in the world. Each year hundreds of firefighters are killed in the line of duty. Thousands are retired early because of job injuries. For this reason, disability retirement benefits are very important to the firefighter. Most communities maintain insurance for the fire department to ensure that there are funds available in case of a job injury that forces an early retirement.

In some cases, the retirement plan covers job injuries. In almost all cases, state laws mandate disability retirement benefits.

## Insurance

A wide variety of insurance programs are available to fire departments. These include life insurance, medical insurance, and sometimes even discounted automobile insurance. The amount of these benefits varies a great deal from department to department, but in almost all cases, the programs selected cover both employees and their dependents.

If a person is injured while on duty, he or she is covered by department disability or retirement funds. Insurance programs are usually set up to help when a person becomes sick or injured while not on duty. These programs are primarily aimed at improving the financial security of the off-duty firefighter. Some cities even have long-term disability insurance. This is a program that helps people restore their incomes to a pre-injury level if they are forced into an early retirement.

## Physical Conditioning

There is a great deal of emphasis on health and safety in this field. Consequently, another of the benefits that the more progressive fire departments offer or require is daily physical conditioning and annual medical examinations. The purpose of the physical conditioning is to keep the firefighters physically fit to perform the fire suppression. The purpose of the annual examination is to identify medical problems before they become a serious threat to the person.

## Allowances

Because the firefighter must be in uniform at all times, uniforms are often dirtied or destroyed. Many fire agencies give each of their members a monthly allowance for the care and maintenance of their work uniforms. The range of these allowances is from $20 to $30 per month; they are often paid quarterly. This allowance is for routine wear and tear only. It is not related to the additional protective clothing that the firefighter uses. In most departments, all protective clothing is paid for and replaced by the agency, according to state law.

## Educational Incentive

Education has become an important aspect of the fire profession. Many departments, to encourage members to gain greater education, offer educational incentives. These may be paid to individuals for different educational achievement levels, or they may be paid to individuals to reimburse them for tuition and books.

They are a real advantage to the person who uses them. Departments that pay educational incentives are often the ones with the greatest potential for promotion. Even where promotions are limited, educational programs are part of the trend toward increased professionalism.

There are limits to these programs. In some cases, the benefit is paid only after completion of specific courses. In other cases, the benefit is for a fixed period of time, and the person must continue to go to school to maintain the benefit.

## *Sick Leave and Vacation*

Like most public and private employees, the firefighter is eligible for sick leave and vacation benefits. The difference in the fire service is that the firefighter's work shift influences the use of the benefits. A firefighter's twenty-four-hour shift means that sick leave and vacation are discharged at the same rate. While in most other jobs a person has a five-day workweek, the firefighter works a twenty-four-hour shift as a part of a team. A member cannot just take a day off when he or she wants to. Vacation schedules are carefully planned in the fire service, and people think twice about using sick leave unless they are really ill.

Because of the shift cycle, it is common for a person to have to work special holidays. Fire never takes a holiday, so the firefighters can't either. This means that they must expect to work some days that family and friends do not. It is sometimes a real inconvenience, and the firefighter cannot expect to have vacation days or take sick leave to compensate for the inconvenience. Most cities pay fire and police personnel overtime for their work when everyone else is off, but they seldom grant special favors on the holidays.

## Intangible Benefits

The fire service has the added benefits of job security, job satisfaction, and personal prestige. These things are not measured in dollars and cents, but they are significant nonetheless.

When talking about job security, most people think in terms of layoffs or reductions in force. The fact is that fire departments in some parts of the country have reduced forces. But that is not what we are referring to in this discussion of security. There are few jobs in which the security of each person is such a concern as it is in the fire service. Firefighters live and work in such a close environment that the teamwork and camaraderie are essential. This translates into a form of security that few other jobs have. Members of the fire service help and look out for each other, just like members of a family do.

Of course, there are exceptions to this image, but they are rare. Job security in this field includes a sense of belonging that transcends the financial aspects of the job.

The second aspect of the job that is hard to define is job satisfaction. When most people finish a day's work, they can go home and almost forget what they did to earn the roof over their head. But after seeing the look on the face of a family member whose loved one you have saved, you realize that being a firefighter is not a workaday job. Its rewards are in the accomplishment of deeds. It pays off in the feelings of satisfaction you get after you have met a challenge and won. There are no price tags for that exhilaration, and there are few other places you can achieve it.

Finally, there is the aspect of personal prestige. The job of the firefighter is regarded reasonably well in our society. Practically every child in the world who visits a fire station wants for a time to be a firefighter when he or she grows up. Those who actually realize that fantasy are often looked upon as being a special kind of person. Many jobs have good public images, but the firefighter is who people call when they are in trouble.

## Summary

Although the pay is respectable, the job benefits match those of other professional occupations, and there is ample job security, firefighters are not in this profession for the money. The benefits they derive come from the camaraderie and great sense of teamwork that exists in the fire service, and from the enormous personal satisfaction that comes from helping save people's lives and property from the devastation of fire.

# 7

# TRAINING AND EDUCATION

EDUCATION HAS NOT always been a high priority in the fire service. There was a time when the basic criteria to become a firefighter were brawn and bravery. That is not true today. Training and education are the backbone of modern fire protection.

Fire fighting has evolved into a complex field that requires a person to be both intelligent and educated in order to do the job. In all probability, this trend will continue. Perhaps it will grow to the extent that a high school diploma will not be satisfactory for competing at the entrance level; some fire departments may require some level of college course work as a prerequisite to employment.

## National Professional Qualifications Board

The National Professional Qualifications Board is probably the best indicator of the evolution of fire fighting into the complex field that it is. This organization sets minimum standards for training and education for various fire service positions. Dr. Leonard

Marks, a deputy chief in the San Jose Fire Department, first suggested the National Professional Qualifications Board in the early 1960s. The board was established and authorized under the Joint Council of National Fire Service Organizations in the early 1970s.

The concept of a set of professional standards was soon introduced to the National Fire Protection Association (NFPA). Currently the NFPA produces four different documents that spell out minimum standards. They are the NFPA 1001 (firefighter), NFPA 1021 (fire officer), NFPA 1031 (inspector/investigator), and NFPA 1041 (instructor).

These standards are used by many fire departments across the country. Several states use the standards as a basis for their certification systems. A complete explanation of the professional qualifications system is available from the National Professional Qualification Board (NFPA, Quincy, Massachusetts 00269).

## High School

A well-rounded education at the high school level is just as important to your potential employment as is the desire to become a firefighter. Good intentions are not enough for one to make good scores on the competitive examinations. There is no special recommended curriculum for individuals interested in this field. The best advice is to make sure that you develop basic skills in reading, writing, mathematics, and other core subjects. Then, if the opportunity presents itself, you should take classes in manual skills, like auto mechanics or building construction. Lastly, if you are so inclined and have the skills, some time should be devoted to competitive sports.

You may now be saying to yourself, "If I could do all of that, I'd go on to college." Well, most entry-level fire fighters do just that. At the outset of employment, they are required to complete rigorous course work at a recruit academy. Most of the material in a recruit academy is about freshman-level college work. But a *D* grade in recruit work means termination of employment.

## Employment to Gain Skills

Another way of getting training that will help you achieve fire service employment is through summer or part-time employment. You would be well advised to seek employment that allows you to use your hands as well as tools—perhaps in a construction, mechanics, landscaping, or masonry job. All of these types of jobs build manual dexterity and strength. Additionally, they help you learn teamwork and how to work under supervision.

## Pre-Employment Training

There are a few opportunities to get some pre-employment training while still in high school. Some fire departments participate in the Fire Explorer program, a career orientation program affiliated with the Boy Scouts of America.

Fire Explorer programs provide a unique set of circumstances for young people between the ages of fifteen and twenty-one to learn about the duties and responsibilities of the firefighter. Explorers receive training in almost every aspect of the service. This often includes such things as fire control, fire prevention, heavy rescue, and emergency medical procedures. In some areas, the Fire Explorers actually respond on fire apparatus as observers during real emergencies.

In many states, Explorer Posts, which are sponsored by fire agencies, annually conduct a Fire Explorer Academy. During that academy, members have the opportunity to meet and work with the same departments that will be selecting new employees in the future. Although the Explorer experience does not guarantee employment, it certainly points out the path to its door.

Another possible source of involvement available in some parts of the country is the Regional Occupational Programs. ROPs sometimes provides career training in fire protection.

# College Education

It is highly unlikely that a student will enter a fire service career directly from high school. The average age of the entry-level firefighter is the mid-twenties. Most departments prefer candidates to be a bit more mature and to have developed a work ethic and some background in the real world. A college education is often helpful.

## Community Colleges

Many community colleges offer fire science courses in subjects such as fire prevention practices, tactics and strategy, hazardous materials, and hydraulics. There is a temptation to jump right into those types of classes if they are available, but it is better to wait.

The best thing to do after high school graduation is to enter a community college and take all of the core classes. Take a few of the courses that will be required for graduation—English, social sciences, and physical sciences. Make an appointment with a counselor and talk about your goals and courses at the beginning of your upper-level educational experience.

If you do take fire science courses, make sure that they are introductory classes. Spend some time talking to the fire science instructors, too. It's not uncommon to find the classes filled with in-service firefighters and a few students. This can create a problem because one group will affect the learning rate of the other.

The problem is not insurmountable, but it has to be recognized. It pays to spend the time to assess the fire science program before getting into it. Getting into classes that were over their heads has devastated many potentially good candidates. In some areas this problem does not exist. The larger fire science programs offer two different courses—pre-employment and post-employment—that separate beginning students from experienced firefighters.

The typical curriculum of a four-semester fire science degree program might have the following core classes:

| Course | Units |
| --- | --- |
| Introduction to Fire Science | 3 |
| Physical Science for Fire Science | 3 |
| Fundamentals of Fire Prevention | 3 |
| Building Construction | 3 |
| Fire Protection Systems | 3 |
| Hazardous Materials | 3 |
| Public Fire Safety Education | 3 |

In addition, the student would be given the option of completing these electives:

| Course | Units |
| --- | --- |
| Fire Management | 3 |
| Fire Command | 6 |
| Fire Investigation | 3 |
| Instructor Training | 6 |

Of course, a student would be expected to complete all of the other academic courses required for a two-year degree. In colleges with extensive fire science curriculums, there are also a variety of degree options ranging from fire administration to fire education. Because of the differences in the electives, one must evaluate each program separately.

Another aspect of pre-employment training that seems to be gaining in recognition is the idea of conducting recruit training prior to the offer of employment. This is often done in cooperation with a community college. These pre-employment academies have prerequisites and very stringent graduation requirements. They are an advantage to the local fire departments because the new firefighter does not have to be trained except in specific departmental practices. They are an advantage to the candidates because it gives them a saleable skill.

## Other College Opportunities

There are several colleges in the United States that specialize in fire protection education. Probably the best known of these is the Fire Protection Technology program at Oklahoma State University. The curriculum at this school is aimed at a fire protection technician level, rather than the firefighter. Graduates of this program are actively recruited by both public and private fire protection agencies.

Additionally, the Oklahoma program offers one of the few four-year degree programs in fire protection. A graduate of this program is not only versed in the science of fire, but also in basic management techniques. The curriculum for this program can be obtained by contacting Oklahoma State University (Fire Technology Department, Stillwater, Oklahoma 70478).

### *Fire Protection Engineering Schools*

There are also schools that provide programs for fire protection engineers. The best of these is the University of Maryland. This program is not designed for entry-level firefighters; it is the best school to look into if you have the mathematical and engineering skills to enter the engineering aspects of fire protection. For more detailed information, contact the University of Maryland (Department of Fire Technology, College Park, Maryland 20742).

## Military Fire Schools

Another option for pre-employment candidates is the Department of Defense's fire service training programs. Many young firefighter candidates have gotten their basic training by entering the military. The obvious advantage to this program is that this schooling is free. It also offers the candidate the opportunity to explore many different facets of fire protection, to travel, and to learn on the job. The disadvantage is the fact that the military service obligation lasts for several years. Sometimes duty assignments are a long way from where you desire to be.

For example, the Air Force Fire Protection Specialists School is nine weeks in length and covers five different blocks of instruction—fire protection objectives and responsibilities; structural fire fighting; operating structural fire fighting vehicles; aerospace vehicle fire fighting; and breathing apparatus, rescue carriers, and first aid. Successful graduates of this course receive five units of college credit from the Air Force Community College.

## Recruit Training

Regardless of a candidate's training and education prior to employment, most fire departments conduct a recruit academy for new personnel. It is like a boot camp for new firefighters. Its purpose is to acquaint the new member to the specific information and techniques used by the local fire department on a day-by-day basis. It is the most crucial training period for a firefighter.

Recruit academies vary in length according to the needs of the local agency; they range from about six to eight weeks. Recruit academies involve intensive mental and physical testing. During that period, the recruit attends classes on topics such as fire behavior, hose handling, raising ladders, tactics and strategy, and rescue and emergency medical skills. Failure to complete the class is usually grounds for dismissal from the department.

During the academy period, the candidate will be evaluated on a variety of things other than grades on tests. The instructors observe candidates to determine their ability to work as part of a team. They will be looking at a person's attitude about discipline and response to orders under stress. Candidates are assessed for their ability to work as a part of a fire company.

Most of a recruit's basic training is done under the supervision of a department training officer. He or she is usually an experienced command officer who not only teaches basic skills, but also relates the information to real emergencies.

Recruit academies are intensive for a good reason. A fire does not care how long you have been on the job. It is not uncommon for brand-new tailboard firefighters to go on a working fire their very first shift. The recruit academy is used to preparing the novice for that eventuality. Knowledge and training are the only defense of a new firefighter. Experience is an unforgiving teacher. That is why the drill instructors in a recruit school press for competency in hose lays, rescue practices, and the wearing of protective devices like breathing apparatus.

Most departments require that new firefighters swear an oath of office at the same time they receive their badges. The combination of pride in graduating from the school, accompanied by the thrill of getting a badge pinned to the new uniform, is something few recruits ever forget.

## In-Service Training

Training and education never stop for the firefighter. If you enter the ranks of the service, you will receive some form of training almost every day you are on duty. Most departments spend a minimum of six to ten hours per month on this task.

Much of the training is repetition of basic skills. This is called drilling. It serves much the same purpose as does drilling on a professional sports team. It keeps basic skills finely tuned for use in high-stress circumstances. Training and drilling are often done under the supervision of the firefighter's direct supervisor, the fire captain.

The second type of training that a firefighter receives is new information. Most modern fire departments have one or more officers designated as training officers. Their job is to bring new information to the department on a frequent basis. Additionally, the training staff and the company officer provide training in improving skills to get individuals ready for promotion. Classes are often held on very specialized subjects like hazardous materials, hydraulics, or leadership and supervision.

Federal laws, complemented by state statutes, often require mandatory training to be conducted on specific areas. Generally these topics deal with either safety or hazardous materials. Mandatory training is very important in reducing the firefighter's exposure to situations that could cause injury or death.

At the bare minimum, however, the in-service firefighter will experience some form of training throughout his or her career. There are almost no exceptions to this rule.

## Specialized Training

Almost all fire service agencies offer a variety of specialized courses once a person completes probation. These courses range from short courses on fire hydraulics and pump operations to extensive ones like officer training or paramedic school. Specialized training is also provided in fields such as fire prevention and fire investigation. As a person is promoted in the fire service, these specialized classes often play an important part in her or his career development.

### State Fire-Training Programs

Most states have a program to help deliver special training classes to local fire departments. In-service personnel often attend state-sponsored schools, seminars, and workshops. Some attend them while on duty, and others have to take off-duty time to attend them. Typical of state fire academies are special courses in flammable liquid fire control, high-rise fire fighting tactics, fire prevention practices, and leadership courses.

If an individual wants to get promoted in the fire service, he or she must attend a combination of internal and external training and education opportunities. Many firefighters start their community college education before they are hired and complete their degrees after employment. Others start going to college after employment and complete requirements so as to prepare themselves for promotional competition. In either case, the combination of resources available from the various states provides an ample opportunity for a person to become competitive for promotion all the way from the tailboard to fire chief.

## *National Fire Academy*

The latest resource that has become available for the fire service is the National Fire Academy. This facility, created by the Presidential Commission on Fire Prevention and Fire Control, is located at Emmittsburg, Maryland. It is currently operated by the United States Fire Administration. Fire officers from all fifty states are selected to attend courses of instruction at the academy on a year-round basis.

Typical of the courses offered at the National Fire Academy are instructor training, computers in the fire service, management of emergency medical programs, and executive development. As you can see, the majority of these courses are aimed at the upper levels of the fire service. There are also courses offered on pesticide fire control, maintenance of fire apparatus, and fire ground management. These are excellent training opportunities for the experienced firefighter.

## Summary

Training and education are an essential part of the fire service. If you are a serious candidate, the best preparation you can engage in is to obtain as much training as possible prior to selection. The more education and training you have already, the more valuable you are to the department. You can be sure that you will be expected to continue your education far into your career.

There is a trend toward certifying different levels of competency in the fire service. This means that before candidates can achieve different levels, they must receive a certain level of training and then be tested to see if they have learned the information. Almost all of the training resources identified in this chapter lead to that process. Another trend at this time is a tendency toward higher levels of education for promotion. Many fire officers today have advanced degrees in such diverse subjects as political science, business administration, and public administration. There is no doubt that a good education will be an important part of the future firefighter's career development.

# 8

---

# FINDING A JOB IN
# FIRE PROTECTION

VERY FEW THRILLS equal the feeling one gets upon being accepted into the ranks of the fire service. It is an old and honorable profession that sets and keeps high standards for its members. To become a part of that experience is reserved for a small segment of our society.

Before you can feel that excitement, you have to get hired. The job of protecting life and property can be a very demanding one; getting hired in order to follow that life goal is often even harder. Becoming a firefighter almost never happens by accident. One must actively pursue a fire service career. There are jobs to be found, but the competition for every position is keen.

For almost every job in the fire service spectrum, there are at least three distinct areas that relate to your finding a job that will meet your needs. These areas are application for openings, testing criteria for the different jobs, and the selection of candidates from those who pass the test. The task of finding a job involves understanding each of these processes and determining how to stay involved in the process long enough to get hired.

## Applying Locally

The best place to start is in your own backyard. The vast majority of jobs in fire protection are local. So you have to tune into the various means that are used to recruit for job openings. When we use the term *recruiting*, it has to be refined a little bit. Seldom do fire fighting agencies have to go out and actively find candidates; when a fire agency says that it is recruiting, it usually means simply that it is accepting applications.

In most people's vocabulary, recruiting implies a widespread search. In the fire service, recruiting usually means selecting new recruits from the people who have already indicated an interest by making themselves available. There are exceptions to this, especially in areas that have been actively involved in dealing with minority hiring requirements. Generally, however, fire agencies do not have to go out and make widespread searches to locate interested parties.

In the urbanized and industrialized areas, fire agencies usually conduct entrance-level tests once a year. This means that a person must be available to take the test when it is offered, or miss the opportunity for employment. Many communities avoid this problem by maintaining a list of interested individuals in their personnel departments.

Therefore, a person interested in a job at a local fire agency should visit all local fire service agencies and determine how to be put on such a list. In the smaller communities, the departments often have the candidates fill out an employment application and put it on file right then and there.

## *The Application*

Sometimes people take the process of filling out an application lightly. But if you are interested enough in the job to take a test for it, you should be interested enough in it to make a good first impression. Fill out the application completely. That means no blank spaces and no unanswered questions. Do it very neatly; it is not necessary that an application be typed, but it should be legible.

In the larger communities, the number of candidates is often so large that keeping all of those applications on file is a problem. These agencies have candidates fill out an interest card. An interest card looks like a postcard. It contains a person's name, address, and phone number. When the department is testing for a position, the card is mailed to the applicant. Usually the interest card will be accompanied by additional instructions about filing applications or appearing for the test date.

There are problems with both the application and interest card systems. It is the responsibility of the interested party to keep the fire agency informed of changes of address or employment status, for example. Most agencies will not spend much time trying to track a person down. If the card or test information returns as "addressee unknown," the card or envelope goes into the wastebasket.

The advantage of this type of system is that a person can be on numerous lists simultaneously without causing a problem. It is an excellent idea to get your name on as many interest lists for tests as possible. In some highly urbanized areas, a person can be on dozens of potential testing lists.

Remember that this is not the type of job for which a person can go and apply directly. It is not uncommon for a department to have hundreds of candidates show up to take out the first applications. In many of the larger cities, they will announce an opening date and a limited number of applications. Candidates often have to set up a vigil just to get applications. There have been cases where candidates have had to wait in line for periods of up to forty-eight hours just to get to fill out an application.

Sometimes a person has to go through a battery or series of tests before learning how to become a successful candidate. Take as many tests as possible to increase your chances of success.

One other suggestion that seems to help candidates is to get a friend or companion with similar interests to take the tests with you. Having a person you can relate to is helpful in the preparation phase of testing. Two or more individuals competing together tend to raise each other's performance levels. It also helps to have someone to discuss tests with.

## Going Beyond the Local Area

If the local market is limited to possible openings, you might have to broaden your horizons somewhat. It is not unknown for a person interested in fire protection to send out postcards to a whole segment of a state to get to the testing phase. The only limit to your search for job opportunities in local fire protection is your own resources in time and money. Because competition is such a keen factor, most fire agencies don't all give their examinations on the same day. Additionally, many fire agencies set up their examinations on Saturdays to give the greatest number of people the chance to compete.

# Beating the Rush for Applications

Another avenue that should be pursued regarding job opportunities in the local situation is that of training programs for paid-call or reserve firefighters. Instead of conducting tests on unknown quantities of candidates, many modern fire departments direct pre-employment candidates to training programs that give them some testing skills. Many community or junior colleges offer classes to prepare applicants for the testing process. Such programs also serve as a resource to locate new job opportunities.

The paid-call or reserve firefighter program is often found in an area that is either undergoing a transition from volunteer to full-time paid fire force or one needing reserves to supplement the paid forces. In those areas, a person can often get into a part-time role that leads to full-time employment. Often these programs closely resemble the internship or apprenticeship programs found in other trades and occupations.

Membership in these types of organizations is not an automatic inroad to employment, however. These programs are also used to weed out people who have a borderline interest. The number of candidates, once again, often exceeds the number of available jobs.

## *Apprenticeships*

In some areas of the country there are apprenticeship programs for which a person can sign up. The apprenticeship program is part of a series of pre-employment training programs developed jointly by the International Firefighters and the International Fire Chiefs associations. There are actually four different programs: firefighter, fire medic, paramedic, and emergency medical technician. The way the apprenticeship program works is that these two organizations form a joint apprenticeship council (JAC) in an area. The JAC has funding to pay an apprentice a small stipend while he or she is going to school.

The program is funded from a combination of local, state, and federal agencies. The training costs are often funded by a combination of local and community college funds.

An apprentice is required to complete a three-year program. The first part of the program consists of the recruit academy. At that time, the apprentice is actually an employee of the JAC. Upon graduation from the academy, he or she becomes indentured to a specific fire agency and is then given the basic wage of that agency and becomes a member of a fire company. For the rest of the three-year agreement, he or she is required to complete a minimum number of hours of training per year.

After completion of the three-year program, the candidate can become a regular full-time member of the agency that he or she has been serving. Apprentices can be removed from service any time during the three-year period if they fail to meet the criteria of the fire agency.

## Applying at the State and Federal Levels

So far we have only dealt with application at the local level. What about those state and federal agencies that employ fire protection personnel? How do they recruit for their employees? Well, the song is very much the same, but the chorus is sung by a larger choir. The number of candidates for state and federal forestry jobs greatly exceeds the demand.

But someone has to be hired, and state and federal governments do it in very much the same way as local government does. They get a list of candidates and conduct tests on them. The way to start in this area is to get a list of the state and federal agencies and send each of them a letter requesting job announcements. Such agencies are often listed in the phone book, or you can get help at your local library. Once again, a person cannot send off one letter and expect immediate success. The correspondence should be directed to every agency with similar job potential.

These jobs are almost always seasonal in nature. That's good and bad. It's good in that there is turnover every year, especially in areas where college students hold many of the seasonal jobs. It's bad in that there is a very narrow hiring window. If you are not selected during that very short period, there is a long wait until the next opportunity.

Some of the job markets at the state and federal levels (discussed in previous chapters) are highly selective. You must be prepared to actively seek them out. Examples of these jobs might be something like the fire agencies that protect military installations. Sometimes these agencies will place job announcements in the local newspaper or post office.

## Employment in the Private Sector

Some of the specialized jobs mentioned in previous chapters really do not recruit. They hire from a labor force different from the fire fighting agencies. Examples are fire extinguisher companies, automatic sprinkler companies, and fire alarm companies. These fields require specific skills, such as knowledge of electronics and mechanics. Therefore, they recruit among people who already have the necessary training in the requisite technical and mechanical skills. Many of the people who enter this trade come from other, related trades. Much of this area of job opportunity involves installing, testing, and maintaining built-in fire protection equipment. The job opportunities are often displayed in the normal fashion of looking for skilled technicians—in newspapers and employment notices.

One of the advantages of this area is that there are often part-time or temporary jobs in these fields. Many people who aspire to fire service careers get job experience by working in the private sector while testing for fire departments.

The major exception to this area is the process used to select the fire protection engineer. Because of the educational requirements of this job and the length of that education process, coupled with a shortage of good fire protection engineers, these people are often individually recruited. It's not uncommon for the graduating class from a good fire protection school to have a list of potential jobs available to them instead of having to look for a job.

## Testing

Getting a job in the fire service is a lot like running the high hurdles on a track team. One has to clear each obstacle to the selection process before moving on to the next one. The normal testing process to get into the fire fighting area of fire protection consists of at least three separate testing procedures. A candidate has to pass each of them separately to become eligible to be hired. These steps consist of a written examination, a physical agility examination, and an oral interview.

## The Written Examination

The written examination is exactly what it sounds like—a series of written questions to measure a candidate's ability to comprehend the work of the fire service. In the past, many of these examinations were difficult to prepare for because they were not well structured. Today, especially after the work that has been done on equal opportunity employment and fair employment practices at the local, state, and federal levels, these examinations are usually closely related to the job.

This means that the questions are aimed at determining if a candidate has the ability to learn the skills of the fire service. The questions relate to a person's ability to comprehend a specific subject area, rather than whether he or she already possesses any knowledge of it.

It is not uncommon for the testing agency to give a candidate a booklet or pamphlet on the subject of fire protection as a reading assignment prior to a written test. The candidate will be given instructions that indicate that test questions will be derived from that specific material. This is legal because it tests a person's ability to learn from a specific body of knowledge. Then when all candidates are tested, they all start with the same basic information.

Frequently, these entrance examinations are prepared by private or government agencies that specialize in the selection process. It is not uncommon for a person to take the entrance examination for several different agencies in the same geographical area and find that the same examination is given. The reason that this can occur is that fire agencies often use standard examinations to ensure testing validity. Another reason that it can occur is that it is cheaper to purchase exams that can be used over and over again than it is to prepare a one-time examination.

This is an advantage and a disadvantage to a test-taker. It is an advantage in that a person can become increasingly familiar with the test instrument and get better and better scores. It is a disadvantage in that the same thing applies to all of the other candidates, too. If you are not getting better scores faster than they are, you lose the competitive edge.

Typically, the written examination will consist of two hundred questions. It will normally take two or three hours. The results of that test may be available in as little as a few days or as long as a month. The difference is based on the practices and procedures of the local agency regarding the scoring of the test papers. If the test is made and scored locally, the time frame is short. If it is a standardized test and has to go back to a central test facility to be scored, it takes longer.

In most cases, the results of the written examination drastically reduce the number of candidates allowed to move on to the next test phase. A cutoff point is often established to limit the number of candidates to a manageable number. It can be as high as 80 percent. In some cases, the testing agency will use a standard passing point, usually around 70 percent. In either case, the written portion results in the elimination of some candidates, usually at least 10 percent.

## Physical Agility Tests

After the written scores have been compiled, the candidates who passed are notified to appear for a series of physical agility tests. These tests gauge a candidate's ability to complete the various strength and maneuvering activities that a firefighter might be asked to perform in the line of duty. These tests have to be job related, too. In the past, fire candidates were asked to perform some unreasonable tasks like hoisting railroad rails and climbing rope ladders to prove agility. Today the tests include such relevant activities as a person's ability to pull a certain amount of fire hose, climb a certain height of ladder, wear an air tank in an enclosed area, and complete a series of physical activities without being totally exhausted.

In the physical agility portion of the testing process, candidates are sometimes given a competitive score that reflects their speed or success at completing the various tasks. In some testing processes, a person is merely given a pass or fail mark on the test. In either case, the result is that the list of candidates gets narrowed once again.

## The Oral Interview

The third test employed by fire agencies is an oral interview. This is basically a discussion with the remaining candidates to evaluate their preparation and potential for the job. Usually the oral board consists of three to five experienced fire officers or personnel officers. Candidates are brought one at a time into an interview room where they are asked a series of questions.

Most of these interview processes are based on a standard interview. All of the candidates are asked the same questions. When the candidates are interviewed, the examiners are limited to asking questions that relate to the qualifications for the job. They are not allowed to ask questions about ethnic, religious, marital, sexual, or political background.

The grading of this process is based on comparing the responses of the different candidates to the same questions. Although there are no standard answers to the questions, the experienced fire officers can make judgments as to the candidates' qualifications for the job. Most fire agencies are looking for characteristics that are job related, such as poise, calmness, self-expression, and ability to follow instructions. The oral board often ranks the candidates from the best to the least qualified in these areas.

The oral interview is the best opportunity you have to sell yourself to the department. The best candidates are just as prepared for this part of the process as they are for the written or physical agility tests. Preparation for the oral interview includes proper dress, a thorough knowledge of the local department's needs and desires, and a sense of self-confidence. You may be asked about why fire fighting interests you, what traits you consider your strengths and weaknesses, and what your goals are for the future, perhaps five or ten years from now. Think about such questions ahead of time so that you will be better prepared to answer them. If there is any one thing that must be emphasized about oral interviews, it is *be yourself.*

The interviewers are trying to find out about that person who is on the other side of the table. They are experts at assessing people. If you try to bluff an oral board or try to create a false image, you will probably do poorly. They know you may be a little nervous; try to relax and pay attention to the questions. Instead of trying to please artificially, just be honest and sincere. Do everything you can to develop poise, tact, and good verbal skills. If you have enthusiasm, self-confidence, and the ability to organize your thoughts, you will do well on oral interviews.

## The Eligibility List and Final Testing

Many fire departments prepare an eligibility list after the basic examinations are completed. This is a ranking of the candidates in order of their cumulative scores from the written, physical, and oral examinations.

The eligibility list is usually good for a period of twelve to twenty-four months after the date the list is posted or distributed. This is done so that the departments will not have to conduct tests too frequently, and yet not so far apart that those candidates will move away before being selected. Usually the list will be exhausted from the highest to the lowest scores. Some departments have policies that the department does not have to follow the list in the selection process. They believe that the list is basically only a means of qualifying candidates, and that one score does not necessarily mean a better candidate than another.

In either case, getting on the eligibility list is still not the same as being hired for the position. Typically the department will select a group of potential employees from the list and put them through another series of tests. These tests are not competitive in nature, but rather are to determine actual fitness for employment. They typically include three steps: a medical examination, a background check, and a final oral interview.

### *The Medical Examination*

The first of these types of exams is a medical examination. Sometimes it is called a physical exam. This is not a scored test. It is an examination by a medical doctor to see if the candidate can perform the job without undue potential for injury on the job. Many fire departments use standard physical exams based on the National Fire Protection Association's Standard 1001. This document identifies minimum standards for such things as cardiovascular fitness, skeletal conformity (backs and joints), ability to distinguish colors, and other vital characteristics.

The physical examination is frequently an area where candidates are badly disappointed in their quest for the job. Many young people have gone all the way through the testing process to find out that they have a congenital heart or back defect that disqualifies them. The only way to avoid that disappointment is to make sure that you have checked to see what the physical standards are and have yourself checked out first by your own physician. Any physician can read NFPA Standard 1001 and determine if there will be a potential problem.

## The Background Check

Another testing process used by some agencies is called a background check. This is a check of the candidate's arrest, credit, and military records. Many departments have discontinued these checks as being discriminatory, but they are still in practice in some areas. The purpose of this clearance is to evaluate fitness for the role of being charged with other people's property and lives. In addition, the clearance is used to make sure that the candidates do not have anything on their records to indicate potential problems performing the basic tasks of the job. An example of this would be a person with a bad driving record who could be prevented from keeping a driver's license.

## The Final Oral Interview

The last hurdle that a candidate often has to clear is the "chief's oral," which is a final oral interview. In smaller departments, this is actually handled by the chief of the department. In larger departments, this task falls to one of the ranking officers charged with the responsibility to select personnel. The purpose of this oral interview is to clarify between the department and the candidate just exactly what is expected of the new employee and to see if there are any last-minute questions or problems.

## Selection

If you have been successful to this point, you may actually get hired! But don't be discouraged if that doesn't happen right away. You could be an excellent candidate and still not get the job because of budget cutbacks. A person can stay on a list for a long time waiting for a call. The ratio of individuals that enter this process compared to those actually hired in the end is about one to twenty. It is not easy to become a firefighter, and in the next decade or so the selection process is likely to get even tougher.

As the old saying goes, "Luck favors the mind prepared." That means that the best way to ensure success in getting selected is to be as well prepared, both physically and mentally, as you can be. One does not get into the fire service simply from desire; there must be a lot of time spent preparing for the competition of the selection process.

## Probation

Just when you were thinking that it was over, the fire service has one more big obstacle for you. Firefighters are not considered as having completed the selection process until they have completed their first year's probation. That means that part of the selection process is the training and shift work that you have to perform during the first twelve months on the job.

Many candidates fail here, too. The percentage of failure is probably down around 2 to 5 percent, but that is still enough to be concerned about. The reason that this probation period is considered to be such a vital part of the selection process is the necessity to evaluate a person's compatibility with others in a living situation and to see how the person deals with stress. There are simply no good tests to prescreen candidates for those characteristics.

During a candidate's probation, he or she will be tested on several different levels—technical, physical, emotional, and personal. Sometimes the department will have a very formal evaluation system for probationary employees. It may include written tests of materials that a probationary firefighter is supposed to learn. In other cases, the evaluation will be much more informal. Usually, however, probationary candidates will know how well they are doing by their interaction with coworkers. In the atmosphere of the fire company, problem people stand out quickly.

## Reserve Programs

Many communities, in an effort to provide better career guidance and a further opportunity to review candidates, have instituted what are known as reserve programs. Reserve programs are essentially part-paid positions that allow individuals to participate in fire department operations without becoming a permanent employee. Communities may utilize the reserve program as a pre-screening device prior to full-time probation.

Many, if not most, of these reserve programs are an outgrowth of departments that make a transition between volunteer and paid departments. On the other hand, a number of communities have instituted reserve programs as a means of cutting down on the total number of candidates. For example, it is not uncommon for several thousand individuals to appear to take an entry-level test. Many communities use the reserve program to determine the level of motivation of an individual aspiring to a fire protection career.

There are two types of reserve programs. In the first of these, called operations reserve, an individual is assigned as an additional person in an engine company or truck company to respond under the tutorage of full-time firefighters. The second type of reserve program is used by some departments for their fire prevention bureaus. In that case, the reserve firefighters are given an opportunity to learn the techniques and responsibilities of fire inspectors. In both cases, the reserve firefighter programs are an excellent opportunity for individuals who have a career aspiration to test themselves against the job.

## Summary

The testing process is long and hard, and it can take several years and numerous entrance tests before a qualified candidate secures a job. The implication of this testing process is twofold. The fire service is looking for good people, not mediocre ones, and the testing process really reduces a group of potential candidates to the most qualified ones. The second implication is that a person can be very well qualified and still take a long time to get to the point of selection due to reasons beyond his or her control. A candidate must be patient and have a sense of purpose and dedication to survive the struggle.

# 9

## PROMOTIONAL OPPORTUNITIES

ONCE PEOPLE HAVE become employed in the fire service, they are on the bottom rung of the career ladder. From that position, they have many options and opportunities in their adult working life. One of the most predictable aspects of the fire service is that it is a function of population. As the population grows, so does opportunity. Because it is a service that is becoming increasingly complex and specialized, it presents many alternatives. If you become employed in this profession, you will have the opportunity to be promoted several times, if you want to be promoted and if you possess the skills and abilities demanded of the different promotional situations. Your first limitation is your own motivation and desire.

Of course, other factors influence the opportunity for promotion, too. The two leading factors that contribute to your chances of getting promoted are growth in the fire agency and turnover in the upper ranks. Growth can result from the geographical area of a department being expanded, from increased population in a department's response area, or from a change from part-time or volunteer firefighters to full-time paid personnel.

Some of the things that could limit promotional opportunity are increased reliance upon built-in fire protection such as automatic fire sprinklers or a shift in population away from the industrialized centers, resulting in less tax revenues to support a department's personnel requirement.

In this chapter, we explore the different career ladders that might be available to you. The fire service has several different tracks to the career ladders because there is a definite need for two different classes of personnel—the generalist and the specialist.

The generalist develops all-around skills in the basic areas of all elements of fire protection. Typical of these positions are line personnel; these are the people who staff the individual fire companies—the firefighters, the apparatus drivers, and the company and battalion chief officers.

A specialist focuses on developing expertise in one area of fire protection. Specialists typically hold staff positions such as fire inspectors, training officers, public education specialists, fire protection analysts, and fire investigators.

## The Generalist Promotional Career Ladder

Once a person has completed probation and been accepted into the position of firefighter, he or she can reasonably expect to spend from three to seven years in that rank. Thousands of firefighters never leave that level and are quite happy about it. While a firefighter, a person may have numerous opportunities to gain special knowledge and skills—for example, to become an emergency medical technician or paramedic while in the firefighter ranks.

Some of these training and education opportunities offer great challenges.

Most generalists aspire to one of the following two ranks sometime within their first ten years on the job.

## *The Apparatus Operator*

The first rank above firefighter, in most departments, is the apparatus operator. This person drives and operates the pumps or aerial ladders on the fire apparatus. In some departments they are called engineers or chauffeurs. They are paid a slightly higher wage than the firefighter because of the added responsibility of driving the apparatus under emergency conditions.

The driver is also responsible for maintaining the truck and performing minor repairs on it. He or she has to be familiar with the operation and design of diesel engines, heavy-duty truck-driving techniques, and the design and operation of hydraulic systems and heavy-duty pumps. The driver is also responsible for calculating and setting the pump pressures on hose lines during a fire fighting situation.

## *The Company Officer*

The second rank above the firefighter is company officer. In some departments this rank is called captain. In others it is called lieutenant. This career position is the supervisor of the respective fire companies. This person manages the time of the others assigned to that company and issues orders and commands at the scene of emergencies. The company officer is a working manager. While he or she commands a crew, he or she also performs many of the fire fighting tasks.

The salary of the company officer is often as much as 25 percent higher than the apparatus operator's salary. This varies according to area, but a company officer can expect to earn close to $45,000 per year.

The company officer has to be familiar with a wide range of knowledge and skill and must be able to train subordinates in the tasks they must perform. He or she must be able to evaluate and discipline the crew and so must be skilled in personnel techniques. He or she must be able to handle a wide range of emergency conditions. This requires knowledge of a wide range of potential solutions to complex problems.

All of these ranks—the firefighter, the apparatus operator, and the company officer—make up the organization of the fire company. A fire company normally consists of three to four people. Each fire company is assigned to a specific piece of apparatus—an engine company, a truck company, or a rescue company. Most communities have a fire company assigned to each fire station in a given area. In some densely populated areas, several fire companies are located in one station. Usually there are at least three shifts of fire crews assigned to each fire company. A shift consists of the basic positions that are assigned to the apparatus for one twenty-four-hour period. Some departments are on a ten- or fourteen-hour shift cycle.

What this means to entry-level candidates is that promotional opportunities at the company level are vertically oriented. For every one or two firefighters in the line, there is an apparatus operator and a company officer directly above. For promotions to occur, the department either must expand by adding new fire companies, or a person must retire. The ratio of firefighters in the fire company to other positions is about even, so promotion can be slow if the department does not grow.

## *The Chief Officer*

In most departments the next position in the promotional ladder is called the chief officer. Depending upon the number of fire companies in a community, there may be a chief officer assigned. The chief officer is the supervisor and leader of the company officers. He or she is responsible for the activities of an entire shift of fire companies. This job consists of a blend of management and administrative details plus responsibility to issue commands on emergencies.

Typically the chief officer is responsible for scheduling, issuing purchase orders, enforcing rules and regulations, and making sure that the various departmental programs are functioning correctly. Most chief officers also assist the fire chief with the budgeting and general management of the department. Most chief officers do not obtain this rank until they have a minimum of five or six years as a company officer.

Salaries for chief officers are usually 10 to 15 percent above the highest paid company officer. Depending on the number of chief officer levels in a department, a person can expect to earn as high as $95,000 per year as a chief officer.

Because one chief officer can supervise as many as five or six fire companies, the ratio of chief officers to the fire companies is low. This means that only the most qualified and competent of the company officers achieve this rank.

Depending on the size of the department, there may be several different levels of chief officer in the line function. For example, in departments with several different battalions, there may be a deputy or assistant chief position to supervise the battalion chiefs.

## The Specialist Promotional Career Ladder

If an individual decides to stay in the line or remain as a general firefighter, the number of promotions can take some time. Some fire personnel opt to learn special skills and therefore increase their job knowledge and promotability at the same time.

The specialist in the fire service has the option of several different career ladders—fire prevention (which includes a subcategory of arson investigation), training, and administration. All of these specializations require combinations of knowledge, skills, and motivation. None of them can be accomplished unless the person makes a conscious effort to get the proper education and experience.

Most of these areas of specialization have the various rank structures we have already discussed. For instance, in the larger fire departments, there are personnel assigned in the fire prevention bureaus with each of the ranks of firefighter, apparatus operator, company officer, and chief officer. The difference is that they do not perform the manual fire fighting functions at all. They are paid to perform different levels of fire inspection or investigation work. Generally, a person can be promoted faster in these jobs because there are fewer people qualified for or interested in these positions. Also, because the specialist has more education, he or she is typically paid 5 to 7 percent more for any respective rank.

The first and most obvious reason most entry-level people are not interested in these jobs is that they are not on the twenty-four-hour shift. Typically specialists work an eight-hour-a-day job, forty hours per week. The second reason is that these positions do not face the daily experience of fire combat. And fire fighting is the main reason many enter this occupation.

However, inasmuch as you are exploring the concept of career development, perhaps you can gain a different perspective here. If you are planning a career in fire service, do not overlook the contributions that staff or specialized jobs do for your promotability. Performing in staff jobs gives you both insight and perspective on the community's fire problems that shift personnel often miss. Additionally, staff personnel are often given the opportunity to really change the nature of the community's fire problems through their day-to-day work. Eliminating a fire problem—saving both lives and property—can be the most satisfying part of the fire profession.

## *The Fire Prevention Bureau*

Positions in the fire prevention bureaus consist of inspectors, public education officers, and arson investigators. The inspector conducts visits to businesses and industries to see if they comply with all of the codes and ordinances. This job often involves detailed understanding of several different sets of laws, a good understanding of human nature, and a comprehensive understanding of such things as building construction and hazardous materials.

Typically, a person with the rank of captain or company officer heads fire prevention bureaus in the smaller fire departments. In the larger departments, this person is often the same rank as a battalion chief. In the metropolitan fire departments, the bureaus may have as many as two or three company officer grades and several chief officers in the structure. The top position in most fire prevention bureaus is the fire marshal.

Public education specialists are usually assigned to work under the direction of the fire marshal. These are the people who work directly with the public to increase the community's knowledge of basic fire prevention practices. They often work with educational programs in the schools or with civic groups. These people have to be skilled at making public presentations. They are often involved in preparing audiovisual aids and working with media representatives. Almost all of these positions are civilian. They seldom have any rank.

The one exception is the public information officer. PIOs are usually found only in the largest fire departments. They are ranking officers assigned to work with the members of the various media. They specialize in dealing with serious emergencies and controversies that arise from time to time. A PIO may be involved in releasing information to the television and newspapers after a major fire has occurred. He or she could be involved in dealing with press releases on the subject of fire code enforcement in highrise structures. These people are usually assigned this task because they have good verbal or written skills and have the ability to communicate effectively.

The arson investigator is another position found in fire prevention bureaus. It is normally a promotion from the inspector position or some other prevention assignment. Arson investigators conduct in-depth investigations of fires and explosions to determine if a crime has been committed. They must be familiar with laws and court procedures. They often have to work in close cooperation with the law enforcement agencies. Arson investigators must have analytical skills and the ability to write comprehensive reports.

## Training Division

Another specialization with promise for upward promotion is the training field. The training officer position in most fire departments is reserved for a person who has the ability to impart both knowledge and technique to the entire department. Often the training officer is involved in the hiring and training of the recruit-level firefighters. He or she is also involved in setting up programs for the respective ranks of apparatus operator and company officer.

In the smaller departments, the training officer is normally the rank of at least captain. In the larger departments, a chief officer holds the position. Depending upon the size of the department, some training divisions have several ranking officers, from captain to assistant chief level.

Training officers can best be compared to teachers. They teach fire fighting. This job is most often given to a person who has already reached the rank of company officer, but who also has the skills and ability to teach or organize training programs. Because training is so important to the safety and effectiveness of the entire department, this job is not treated lightly. It usually is assigned to a person who exhibits the ability to be promoted in the near future.

## *Administrative Positions*

In the larger departments, there are often positions that cannot be classified into any of the other categories already discussed. One such category of ranking positions is administrative. Typically administrative positions are at the chief officer level. Many departments are creating civilian administrative positions, but the pay is in the same salary range as that of the chief officer.

Administrative positions concentrate on the completion of tasks that are neither combat nor specialty oriented. Typically, these jobs involve high-level management or financial skills. They involve things such as budget control, personnel matters, and completing staff reports for the chief of the department.

Although administrative jobs don't sound exciting on the surface, they are often among the most difficult in the field. The reason they are so difficult is that the administration of any governmental agency requires a rare blend of technical expertise in management with strong negotiating skills. In the modern fire service, administrative positions are frequently the key to adequate funding and resources for a fire department. These positions are often the ones that have the facts to support justification of the department's different programs.

## The Fire Chief

Probably every child has fantasized at one time or another about being the fire chief. Every year, hundreds of thousands of red plastic fire helmets appear under Christmas trees. Yet, less than one out of every thousand people who enter the fire service will ever be promoted to the rank of fire chief.

The reasons are many. The primary one is that it takes a combination of knowledge, experience, motivation, and personal sacrifice to become a fire chief. Not everyone who enters the fire service has that combination. Not everyone who has that combination is in the position to utilize those talents. And competition for the position can often be very strong.

In the past few years, there has been a noticeable shift in the selection of fire chiefs. At one time, most fire chiefs were merely the oldest, most experienced firefighters. That is not true today. Most of the individuals selected today are well-educated, well-rounded, and professionally mobile people. Most of the current chief officer candidates are people who have served in many different capacities ranging from combat to specialist roles. It is not uncommon for the fire chief candidate to have a minimum of a bachelor's degree, with many having master's degrees.

Most of the individuals who achieve the rank of fire chief are well versed in both technology and good management techniques, with the emphasis on management. The average time in the service to achieve this position is hard to assess. It varies from one part of the country to the other, but it is in the area of twenty-five years of service.

The salary range of the fire chiefs is wide. In the smaller communities, it may be as little as 10 percent over the next highest-ranking officer. In the large cities, the fire chief can earn as much as $125,000 per year. The national average is about $85,000 per year.

The job of the fire chief is diverse. He or she must manage the resources of the department to reduce the loss of life and property from a wide range of emergencies. He or she is required to be reasonably familiar with the general and special fire protection knowledge used by subordinates.

## Summary

Promotional opportunities in the fire service are somewhat difficult to project. On the one hand, we can expect to see an increase in the number of professional firefighters in the future. Fire protection is a product of growth, and as communities grow, so will the fire service. Yet the growth will not be directly proportionate. We can predict that there will be an increased emphasis on education for promotion in the fire service. Cities and towns will probably have fewer firefighters per every thousand people than there were over the past few decades. But government will probably pay the firefighters better and place more emphasis on professionalism. We can expect to see improved techniques developed for future fire protection personnel, which may influence both entry and promotional opportunities.

As a potential candidate for a career in the fire service, you will be well advised to study the direction that the fire service in your area seems to be heading. Talk to the ranking officers in the local fire department and get their opinions on the growth potential of the department. Study the courses of instruction that are being attended by the in-service fire personnel to get some idea of the areas of expertise that are being developed.

In the final analysis, a person's career is a combination of two different factors—preparation and potential for promotion. Preparation is up to the individual. Potential for promotion is often a factor of being prepared at the right time. As you enter your career, you may not be able to set your goals too high. But don't fail to eventually set your goals somewhere. The future of the fire service belongs to those who have a career plan. Someone has to be in charge of every fire department. It might as well be the person best prepared for the role, and that could be you.

# 10

# THE FUTURE OF
# FIRE PROTECTION

IN THE FUTURE, fire service personnel will have to do more work with less help; therefore, productivity will be an important worker trait. There will be increasing emphasis on built-in fire protection devices. Electronics and computers will be just as important to the firefighter as water, hose, and ladders. More personnel will be slotted into staff or specialized positions. Many of these positions will be civilian. Many of the future jobs in the fire service will not be for combat-oriented, suppression personnel. There will be more emphasis on education and certification for promotion.

Fire fighting apparatus will probably get smaller, more like the attack pumpers of today. Fire departments will probably be more involved in research and development of chemicals to fight fire, such as foams, gels, and water additives.

Equipment is likely to get lighter and lighter. This may mean that emphasis on the physical aspects of fire fighting will be replaced by an increasing emphasis on a person's mental capabilities. Personnel will be expected to think their way through the challenges. This will probably result in even more emphasis on certification, training, and education for individuals before promotions in the fire service. This could have the effect of drawing a line of distinction in the fire service between the entry-level personnel and the officers. Those who have the education and knowledge will be promoted faster than those who do not.

## Productivity and Performance

Productivity and performance will probably be the battle cry of the future. Current trends toward tax reform and reduction of the total amount of funds devoted to government may result in more fire protection services being taken over by private enterprise. Those areas that still want the government to be responsible for fire protection may seek ways of reducing overhead costs. This could result in the consolidation of several different fire agencies into superagencies. Smaller fire agencies may see the necessity of forming joint-powers agreements or regionalizing into one large fire department.

An emphasis on the concept of standards may result in the adoption of entry-level standards all across the country. NFPA Standard 1001 may form the basic criterion in every fire agency. This could also cause the examinations and minimum standards for promotion to become more standardized from department to department. As a result, a person may have the opportunity to move from one community to another with no loss of seniority or benefits. This concept of professional mobility may result in a class of professional officers with privileges like those exercised by executives in private enterprise.

Increased professionalism and standards of education could result in more uniform application of principles and theory. But that does not mean that all fire agencies will be alike in practice or procedure. Communities will retain the sense of identity that makes it necessary to create fire protection customized to a particular area. Our cities will not change, but our approaches to their problems will. We will probably see a wide spectrum of customized fire protection.

Based on more effective use of data, fire agencies will develop a basic approach that mandates that if there is to be a standard, it will be to provide a level of service that is economically correct for the local fire problem. Fire protection may take on the trappings of a business function. It may become much more sensitive to factors such as local tax bases and insurance program payoffs.

The most obvious thing that will result from all of these endeavors is that there will probably be a net reduction in the total resources a community will devote to fire protection. This may frighten those who are in service at the time and may result in labor turmoil in the future.

## Offense Versus Defense

Avoiding the catastrophic theory of reform has always been a goal of the fire service. In the future, it may become a realistic goal. As a result of more careful planning and the analysis of data on fire problems, the fire service may have the opportunity to go from a defensive posture to a more aggressive one. Already fire chiefs, fire marshals, fire inspectors, and other staff members are taking strong leadership roles in city planning and in community policies on land use.

As the fire problem becomes more manageable, there may be a reduction in number of fire companies and in the number of suppression personnel. This may be offset by an increase in fire inspectors, training staff, public education personnel, and computer operators. With the emphasis shifting toward reducing the combustibility of the environment, jobs in the functions of consultation, plan-checking, inspection of built-in facilities, and research and development may pay more than do those for firefighters.

The immediate future may not see the development of the completely fireproof structure, but land use and the need for low-cost housing may cause more densely built housing developments and an increase in prefabricated structures. And prefabricated homes may be required to be built from self-extinguishing materials that are both low in cost and strong enough to resist fire.

There may well be an increased emphasis on the writing of codes and ordinances to better control the fire problem. Accidental fire may someday be considered an act of negligence. Spiraling costs of construction and insurance rates, and the depletion of natural resources, may make current levels of fire loss unacceptable. This may lead to the necessity for much more rigid enforcement of fire codes than are tolerated by society today. This may cause an increase in either private or public sector fire inspection activities.

## Complexity of the Fire Problem

The fire problems of the future will become more complex. Even as we predict an increased emphasis on fire prevention and a decreased emphasis on combat personnel, we must note that fire fighting may become even more hazardous. Conditions today point to that possibility.

Changes in energy sources could increase fire risks. Hydrogen and nuclear power may become major sources of energy to replace fossil fuels. Solar energy also can create problems if the solar heating units are improperly installed. Hydrogen and liquefied gases may someday come to be used as vehicle fuels. This could greatly increase the danger from a simple incident such as a vehicle fire.

Hydrogen is a gas. To be used as fuel, it has to be condensed into a liquefied form and stored. When hydrogen is stored like that, it is called a *cryogenic*. Cryogenic liquids are very cold, and if a cylinder ruptures, the gas instantly vaporizes. You cannot control its flow as you can a gasoline leak. Hydrogen is also a tiny molecule that can leak out of the smallest opening possible. Once hydrogen is in the atmosphere, it has an explosive range from 4 to 75 percent. When it burns, the flame temperature is nearly 3500 degrees Fahrenheit, and the flame is almost invisible.

Even if nuclear and hydrogen power do not evolve, there probably will be synthetic fuels to replace the gasoline and diesel fuel of today. The fuel may be a solid fuel pellet, or it could be a chemical that creates new problems we cannot yet even imagine.

## Changes in Fire Service Jobs

Combat personnel may change, too. Fires will continue to occur. Firefighters will always be required to fight them. The infantry nature of the fire service will probably always be with us, but it may be different. Inasmuch as personnel costs are the major part of any fire service budget, there will be an emphasis on productivity in the combat ranks. Salaries are constantly increasing, and tax bases are stretched to the limit in many places, so the firefighter of the future may be expected to be many more things to many people.

The workweek may decrease, and the current practice of having fire companies on twenty-four- or ten- or fourteen-hour shifts may disappear. However, fire personnel may become even better paid and the fringe benefits become even better than they are today. Instead of becoming highly specialized in the task of fire combat, the future firefighter may become more of a generalist. As the specialists take on more and more of the technical sides of built-in fire protection, the combat firefighter may have to become more involved in the people service. Someday all firefighters may be qualified as either emergency medical or paramedical personnel. At the very least, certification will be expected at basic levels of competency in emergency services.

## Preparation and Testing

Future professional firefighters may select their careers while they are still in high school or at least by the time they have reached the age of twenty-one. This may be required because of the mental and psychological parameters that will be set forth for entry into the profession. Preparation for entrance into the fire service will have to be even more deliberate than it is today.

Testing for candidates' abilities and interests will be used to direct personnel into one of two curricula. Not unlike the medical and legal professions today, a candidate may become a paraprofessional or technician if he or she does not appear to have the credentials to handle the more difficult curriculum. Others may be selected to become the professional and receive a more difficult educational path. The choice may be made by the individual or by the entry-level requirement. In either case, we can expect fire service agencies to become more interested in counseling future personnel. This may even extend into the providing of sponsorships or scholarships to attend specified colleges and schools.

Identification of basic knowledge and abilities coupled with intensive pre-entry training and education may result in the almost total disappearance of on-the-job training, as we know it today. The probationary candidate of tomorrow may come from technical school and already be prepared to function; the well-educated cadet fresh from a state or national fire academy may simply step into the ranks.

## Increased Computer Use

That doesn't mean that firefighters will stop their continual training. To remain current with technological changes, the fire service of the future will probably use computer-driven teaching machines to inform personnel of new material. Utilizing individualized training and education files, fire personnel will review old material and be updated as needed. As the computer acquires information about a particular person, there will be little need for repetition. In-service training will be almost entirely directed toward acquiring new skills and knowledge. Periodic reviews of a person's file by her or his superior may replace performance evaluations.

The use of computers will not be restricted to tutoring fire personnel. With the computer's ability to store, retrieve, and manipulate data, it will become a prime tool of the fire manager in the future. Computer-driven management information systems, some of which are in use today, will multiply into total documentation systems to dwarf today's efforts. Besides recording and reporting data, they will be used to predict or simulate fire problems and then analyze different ways of dealing with them. They will become a big part of the decision-making process of the future fire officer.

### Increased Use of Aviation

Continued advances in the use of aircraft in response to wildland fires and helicopters for use in emergency medical service may open up a new field of aviation with a fire service emphasis.

## Implications for the Future

We study the past of the fire service to learn a little bit about the history and traditions of a proud occupation. We study the present to learn about the way things are today. We study the future to survive. Today's fire apparatus is beautiful, chrome-plated, and powerful, but it could be a dinosaur in a few years. Its electronic siren is a far cry from the clanging of the bell on a steamer. Yet only a few life spans cover the transition from horsepower to diesel power. The question now is, "What does the future hold for the fire service?"

The way we fight fire will change, but the burden of responsibility will not. You will have an opportunity to participate in that change. The challenges you will face will be big ones. The changes you will witness will be controversial and dynamic. You can choose to be part of the change or to resist, but it will happen nonetheless.

There are some real problems in accurately predicting the future. Technological and sociological changes occur so rapidly that accuracy in forecasting the distant future is limited. At best, predictions of the future are restricted to anticipating change created by factors and conditions that are part of our knowledge today.

As a future member of the fire service, you ought to consider seriously the possibilities of change. It could affect your preparation for the job. It could affect your desires for the job. It could affect your actions once you have gotten into the service. You need to consider the future because that is where you will play out all of the realities of a career that will either be a satisfaction or a disappointment to you.

## Summary

Today the future looks bright. The fire service promises to continue to be a challenging and rewarding profession. Increasing emphasis on public awareness of fire prevention ensures that the services of firefighters will continue to be respected, especially as fire service personnel raise their own standards of competence and education. If you become one of the select people to enter the fire protection service, you will indeed have a career to be proud of.

# 11

## SOURCES OF
## ADDITIONAL INFORMATION

SO FAR IN this book we have explored many facets of the field of fire protection, but we may have also created questions in your mind. It is impossible to write a book to cover every possible detail. You will have to get a lot of specific answers to your questions before you can move ahead in the selection of a fire service career.

The purpose of this chapter is to give you an overview of sources of information that will have the up-to-date details on the subjects of employment opportunities, training and education, and changes in the field. You may not have the time or money to explore all of these resources, but access to some of them is as simple as going to the local fire station and asking to see a recent copy of a publication.

Wherever possible, we offer a brief description of the organization, what its basic purpose is, a mailing address, and the names of its publications. Many of these organizations change from time to time, but most of the national organizations have been in existence for decades and should be reasonably easy to contact.

What this means to you in your research is that even though local organizations may be the closest to you, they may be the most difficult to utilize unless you have the assistance of someone from the local fire department. And the national organizations may be the easiest to locate, but the most expensive to use. How far you will go to utilize these resources depends on your own resources and how serious you are in the pursuit of a job.

## Local Organizations

One of the best resources available is the closest fire station. Generally, all you have to do to start getting information about the local fire department is ask. Firefighters tend to be very proud of their occupation. They are usually hospitable to people who express an interest, but that doesn't mean that they will let you monopolize their time. To get the most out of the local resources and not wear out your welcome, the following suggestions are good guidelines.

### Phone First

Obtain the local fire department's business telephone number. Make sure that the number is for regular business and not for emergencies. After obtaining the number, call up and ask for the office of the fire chief. It is not necessary that you talk to the chief in person. The reason you call that office is to ask the secretary for information on the department's hiring practices. You should be courteous and brief in your request. Be prepared to provide a complete mailing address.

Don't be surprised if the secretary refers you to another office or even to another department, such as personnel. That's why you are better off making the initial call by phone instead of in person. The larger the department, the more likely you will be sent to someone else to get the details. The reason you start with the chief's office is that it cuts down on false leads to the correct person.

After you get the basic hiring package, review it thoroughly. You should become familiar with all the details of the testing procedures and necessary qualifications. In some cases, the only thing that the local department will provide is a job description or flyer. In other cases, you will receive a large amount of information. In either case, read it from cover to cover.

## *Visiting a Station*

After you have accomplished that chore, locate the closest fire station to where you live. Or, if your town or city has only a few stations, find out where the fire headquarters is located. Call the department and ask to speak to one of the following people: the station captain, the on-duty company commander, or the department training officer. Any of these three people can be helpful to you. Once you have made contact with one of them, ask for an appointment at a specific date and time. The best time for most fire officers is between 4:00 and 5:00 P.M. on the weekdays. In some cases, weekends are better if the officer is on a shift schedule.

Keep the appointment. Punctuality and discipline are very important in the firefighter's world. If you make an appointment and fail to keep it, forget about getting another one. If you must cancel the date, call well in advance and let the person know what your problem is. Conversely, if you arrive at the scheduled time and the person is not there, sit down and wait. He or she may be on an emergency response.

Ask the person to give you a brief description of the department's hiring practices, including a brief overview of the testing process. He or she will not give you any specific information about the questions on the test, but will discuss general practices and procedures. After you have discussed hiring practices, collect as much information as you can about the department's vital statistics—the number of personnel, fire companies, hiring rates over the last few years, potential for growth, and any other pertinent information.

Take good notes and have your questions prepared in advance. Fire officers are often very busy people, so it is a good idea to conclude the interview in about one to one-and-a-half hours. That is about all that the officer can afford to give you.

If you have done your homework well and have prepared yourself to ask the right questions, you will be able to leave the station with a good idea of what to expect. Depending on the size of the department, you might want to take an additional step. A visit to one of the fire stations to talk to the actual firefighters can be a helpful experience. Once again it is a good idea to call in advance and schedule the visit for a predetermined time. Conduct the session carefully and have a cut-off time.

Through this technique, you establish a relationship with a member of the fire service. This can often be a tremendous advantage because of the counseling that a candidate can get from an in-service person. This is sometimes referred to as mentoring; it is a form of counseling and personal guidance. Mentors won't do anything illegal or unethical for you, but they will help you get prepared for the testing process.

## *Inquiries by Mail*

Sometimes a person cannot do these things locally. If you live in a rural area where jobs are scarce, you may have to do the same thing by a combination of telephone and mail. The same point should be made about telephone and mail inquiries regarding your starting point. Start your inquiry at the fire chief's level. After calling to find out the chief's name, write him or her a short, complete note requesting hiring information. Make sure that the note is properly prepared regarding spelling, punctuation, and grammar. Be sure to include a stamped, self-addressed envelope for the return of the information.

## State Agencies

The number and type of potential fire service positions vary dramatically from one state to another. The greatest number of potential jobs at the state level seems to be in the western and the southeastern parts of the country because of the ground covers. However, almost every state has some fire protection employment opportunities.

There are several ways to check out the potential for these jobs. The first way is an extension of the methods suggested for the local level. This method employs the use of the fire service itself. In almost all of the states there is a state fire chiefs' association. This is usually a private organization consisting of fire chiefs who gather together to work on fire service–related problems. There is almost always a state fire marshal or state fire training program. These are usually a function of the state government vested with the job of enforcing fire codes or providing training to the fire departments. In either case, they are well qualified to evaluate employment opportunities.

Your local fire department will usually have the address of the state fire chiefs' association. Ask for the mailing address of the business office or the current secretary of the association. Then draft a letter to that person asking for assistance in doing two things. The first is to get a copy of the mailing address of association members. This will help you locate other possible municipalities that are hiring. The second is to ask the person for information on the addresses of organizations that provide fire protection services.

Write a similar letter to the office of the state fire marshal or the director of state fire training, asking for information on how to locate the state agencies that provide fire protection jobs. Also ask for the name and address of the state employment office. Even if the state agencies do not have entry-level positions themselves, they should know about the other agencies. You will have to write or telephone the specific agencies to get more detailed and current information.

## Federal Agencies

While the employment outlook for all fire protection careers is generally favorable for the future, the number of positions in the federal government engaged in fire protection is especially favorable. One reason for this is that many of the federal fire positions are seasonal.

There are two ways of getting information about federal jobs. The first is to contact the agencies directly. The second is to stay in touch with the state employment office, because it posts information on federal job opportunities. The U.S. Office of Personnel Management maintains thirty-nine federal job information centers around the country. Most of these are located in larger cities.

Contacting a federal job information center can be an effective way of looking into opportunities. These centers not only post announcements, but also may provide information on general qualifications, testing information, and hiring criteria for the entire federal system. If you cannot get to the job center in person, you may contact it by telephone or by mail.

Contacting the agencies that provide fire protection directly is the most effective way to assess job opportunities, but there are limitations. Contact as many of these agencies as possible to get the criteria for employment, and then set your focus on one or two of the agencies to approach.

The best agencies to start with in the federal fire service are:

U.S. Forest Service
Department of Agriculture
Washington, DC 20240

Bureau of Land Management
Department of Agriculture
Washington, DC 20240

U.S. Park Service
Department of Interior
Washington, DC 20240

Department of Defense
Washington, DC 20240

## Nationally Recognized Sources of Information

Because the fire service is so diversified, it requires many organizations and resources to continue to function. Some of these organizations can be very helpful to the aspiring firefighter. The following is a brief list of the major fire service organizations you might contact to get more information. None are recommended as sources of employment; rather, they are listed as sources of information on preparing for employment, or for information on the career potential.

National Fire Protection Association
Batterymarch Park
Quincy, MA 02269

The NFPA, as it is commonly called, is the largest private organization involved in fire protection. This group publishes most of the standards used by the fire service as well as many publications that are helpful to the specialty fields in fire protection. One of the most important standards that it publishes related to career opportunities is the Medical Standards for Entry Level Firefighters, NFPA 1001. It also publishes a variety of magazines and newsletters that contain useful information, such as *Fire Journal* and *Fire Technology*. Frequently there are job announcements in the advertising sections.

The NFPA is divided into sections. Each section specializes in one area of fire protection. When a person joins the NFPA, he or she is invited to join one of these sections to receive different types of information. Four sections of interest to a person researching a career are fire service, fire marshals, fire educators, and Society of Fire Protection Engineers.

International Fire Service Training Association
Oklahoma State University
Stillwater, OK 74078

This organization, usually referred to as IFSTA, is primarily designed to produce training materials for the fire service. Although the bulk of the material is aimed at the in-service person, IFSTA does produce several good publications that can aid a person looking for employment. Several of its publications are aimed at reviewing basic skills a candidate might need to brush up on. Examples of these publications are *Mathematics for the Fire Service, Chemistry for the Fire Service*, and the textbooks that are used by most of the recruit academies. IFSTA also publishes a newsletter called *Speaking of Fire*, which contains useful information on fire service careers.

International Association of Black Professional Fire Fighters
8700 Central Ave., Ste. 306
Landover, MD 20785

The aims of the IABPFF are to identify and correct any injustices in working conditions and to promote interracial recruitment and advancement of competent African-American firefighters within the fire service.

International Association of Firefighters
1750 New York Ave. NW
Washington, DC 20006

The IAFF is the largest firefighters' organization in the country. It is a labor organization that represents the needs of its membership. It can often direct a candidate toward career opportunities. The IAFF is active in the development of apprenticeship and pre-employment programs. The IAFF does not produce many publications of general interest, but it is usually cooperative in helping find information for anyone who asks.

International Association of Fire Chiefs
4025 Fair Ridge Dr.
Fairfax, VA 22033-2868

The IAFC is the organization that represents fire chiefs on matters relating to legislation, training, and education. Obviously, being a fire chiefs' organization, it is not designed to function for the entry-level person. Yet in many ways it is among the most important of the groups, for the fire chiefs are the ones who prepare and defend the budgets of the fire departments.

The IAFC will send out information on career opportunities in the fire service. Also, the IAFC has been instrumental in sponsoring things such as the Fire Explorer program and many of the educational opportunities that assist pre-employment personnel. The primary publication of the organization is aimed almost exclusively at the fire chief and has limited value to pre-employment individuals.

International City/County Management Association
1120 G St. NW
Washington, DC 20005

The majority of firefighters in this country work for cities and counties. The organization with the best overview of employment in the public sector is the ICMA.

This organization each year publishes the *Municipal Year Book*. The yearbook is based on research done to determine salaries and benefits for a wide range of reasons. Among the facts collected from local jurisdictions are elements that could be helpful in job searching, such as information on the size and type of fire departments, the number of employees, the starting salaries and benefits, and the total department budgets. You need not buy the yearbook just to read this information. Most good public or college libraries should have it.

Women in the Fire Service, Inc.
P.O. Box 5446
Madison, WI 53705

The purpose of WFSI is to actively encourage the recruitment, participation, and advancement of women in the fire service by providing information and resources, creating networks, advocating for change, and developing policy guidelines.

American Emergency Services
P.O. Box 215
Wheaton, IL 60189

American Emergency Services is a private provider of fire protection and emergency medical services. It is a source of information regarding private sector involvement in a wide variety of activities.

Association of Public Safety Communications Officials
P.O. Box 669
New Smyrna Beach, FL 32069

For those who want to consider the field of fire service communications, APCO is an excellent resource. It distributes information relating to the practices and procedures used in fire and police dispatch centers. Although APCO itself does not hire personnel, it could be helpful in locating entry-level positions through canvassing member organizations.

International Association of Wildland Fire
P.O. Box 2100
Skokie, IL 60077-7800

This organization focuses on issues affecting wildland fire agencies. The major emphasis in this organization's focus is on policy and research, but there is information in the magazine for the operational members of the fire service to use.

Canadian Association of Fire Chiefs
L'Association Canadienne des Chefs de Pompiers & Prevention des
    Incendies du Canada
1-2425 Pron Don Reid
Ottawa, ON
Canada K1H 1A4

The CAFC is an independent, nonprofit organization with voluntary membership dedicated to reducing the loss of life and property from fire and to advancing the science and technology of the fire service in Canada.

# Publications

Another good way of being current in the field of fire protection is to subscribe to one of the professional publications that are distributed to the fire service. These magazines contain a variety of articles that range from the very technical to the basic. Many fire science students subscribe to one or more of them long before they are employed. It helps to build a vocabulary, gain insight into the workings of the profession, and discover trends in employment opportunities. Although few departments advertise entry-level jobs in these magazines, many advertise promotions and specialty jobs. Usually a department that is promoting people is hiring people.

Among the best of these magazines are:

*American Fire Journal*
9072 E. Artesia Blvd., Ste. 7
Bellflower, CA 90706

*Fire Chief Magazine*
330 N. Wabash Ave., Ste. 2300
Chicago, IL 60611

*Fire Engineering Magazine*
875 Third Ave.
New York, NY 10022

*FireHouse Magazine*
82 Firehouse La., Box 2433
Boulder, CO 80321

*Wildfire*
4025 Fair Ridge Dr., Ste. 300
Fairfax, VA 22033-2868

## Websites

The Internet is a popular place today to conduct research on specific topics. It is virtually impossible to post all of the websites that will be of use to those looking for specific information. However, most of the organizations mentioned in this text, as well as the organizations that support the fire service, have started up websites to keep their information current. Start with this list and build upon the links that become available.

iafc.org: International Association of Fire Chiefs
cfainet.org: Commission on Fire Accreditation
   International and the Commission on Chief Fire
   Officer Designation
iaff.org: International Association of Firefighters
http://iawfonline.org: International Association of
   Wildland Fire
ifsta.org: International Fire Service Training Association
cfsi.org: Congressional Fire Services Institute
fireforceone.com: Fire Force One
firechief.com: *Fire Chief* magazine

## Summary

The more research that you do about the fire service, the greater your chances of employment become. One must have the minimum qualifications just to compete. Those who succeed are almost always the ones who take that little bit of extra time to learn something more.

The sources identified in this chapter are like windows into a house. One cannot enter the house through the windows. Yet by looking into those windows you can gain insight that will help you walk through the door. Many of the sources that we have identified here will lead you to other resources. Use them to your advantage.

# Bibliography

The following books and pamphlets may be helpful as extra reading on the subject of fire protection.

*Brotherhood.* Ogilvy and Mather. American Express, 2001.

Delsohn, Steve. *The Fire Inside.* New York: Harper-Collins, 1996.

*Essentials of Fire Fighting.* IFSTA 200. Stillwater, Okla.: International Fire Service Training Association, 1998.

*Faces of Ground Zero.* Life Books. New York: Little, Brown and Company, 2002.

*Firefighter Professional Qualifications Standard 1001.* Quincy, Mass.: National Fire Protection Association.

*Firefighters: Stories of Survival from the Front Lines of Firefighting.* Edited by Clint Willis. New York: Thunder Mouth Press, 2002.

*Orientation and Terminology. IFSTA 202.* Stillwater, Okla.: International Fire Service Training Association, 1993.

Richardson, George J. *Symbol of Action: A History of the International Association of Fire Fighters,* Washington, D.C.: IAFF, 1974.

Smith, Dennis. *Report from Engine Company 82.* New York: McCall Books, 1972.

# About the Author

Ronny J. Coleman is currently the president of the Fire Emergency Training Network (FETN) and is the chairman of the board of the Commission on Fire Accreditation (CFAI). This organization also operates the Chief Fire Officer Designation program (CFOD). From 1992 to 1998, he served as the state fire marshal and chief deputy director for the California Department of Forestry and Fire Protection, a position he had been appointed to by California Governor Pete Wilson.

Chief Coleman previously served as fire chief in the cities of Fullerton and San Clemente. Prior to that he served as operations chief of the Costa Mesa Fire Department. During his tenure in the fire service he has served in every rank, starting as a wildland firefighter in the U.S. Forest Service, spending time as a supervisor of fire control for the National Park Service, and then becoming a municipal firefighter. Before becoming fire chief, he spent time in every rank from probationary firefighter through apparatus operator, fire inspector and investigator, captain, battalion chief, training officer, and then operations chief.

Most of his career has revolved around training and education. After appointment as a captain in Costa Mesa, he became a recruit academy coordinator, then a fire science instructor for the community college fire science program. Chief Coleman has subsequently taught at every level of the fire service training and education system. This has included working with the Fire Explorer program (affiliated with the Boy Scouts of America), high school Regional Occupational Programs (ROPs), community colleges, state universities, the National Fire Academy at Emmittsburg, Pennsylvania, and international events.

After receiving an A.A. in fire science in 1973, he completed a B.A. in political science from the California State University at Fullerton. He was recently awarded a master's degree in vocational education from California State University at Long Beach, where he was also recognized as a 1995 alumni of the year.

Early on in his career, Chief Coleman participated in the development of a UCLA research project entitled "Study of a Fireman's Occupation." This resulted in his involvement in the creation of the state's first Master Plan of Training and Education. He once oversaw the California Fire Academy and certified individuals who completed the process outlined in that plan.

In 1978 Chief Coleman wrote *Management of Fire Service Operations*, a college textbook on the subject of fire ground management. Since then he has written many more textbooks covering subjects as diverse as residential fire sprinkler systems, hazardous materials terminology, and the history of fire protection technology development. Between 1988 and 1989 he served as the president of the International Association of Fire Chiefs. In 1992 he was elected as the first North American fire chief to serve as a vice president to the International Technical Committee for Fire Protection, an organization that represents about forty different nations in the field of fire protection.